Cryptocurrency
Risk Management

A guide for family
wealth managers

JOSHUA M. PECK

R^ethink

First published in Great Britain in 2023
by Rethink Press (www.rethinkpress.com)

To my wife and children, my greatest blessing;
and to all families who choose prosperity

Disclaimer

While the publisher and author have used their best efforts in preparing this book, they make no representations or warranties with respect to the accuracy or completeness of the contents of this book and specifically disclaim any implied warranties of merchantability or fitness for a particular purpose. None of the information in the book should be construed as legal, investment, or tax advice. This book is for educational purposes only and is not a substitute for any sort of professional legal, investment, or tax advice. Neither the publisher nor author guarantees the success of any action you take in reliance on the statements contained herein and they shall not be liable for any loss of capital or other damages, including but not limited to special incidental, consequential, or other damages, resulting therefrom.

The reader should note that any investment involves a high degree of risk, including loss of principal. Past performance of any strategy is not indicative of future results and all investments involve risk of loss. This book cannot and does not guarantee or predict any outcome with respect to any investment. The author makes no implications, warranties, promises, suggestions or guarantees whatsoever, in whole or in part, that by participating in any investment the reader will earn any money whatsoever.

Furthermore, any description herein of the author's strategies is based purely on the empirical knowledge of the author and should not be considered definitive or a guarantee that the strategies mentioned will, in fact, succeed. Performance results and examples of risk mentioned in the book are presented for information purposes only. The risks outlined herein are not a complete enumeration or explanation of all risks involved when investing in digital assets and cryptocurrencies, and readers should conduct their own independent investigation and consult with professional advisors of their choosing for a more complete understanding of the risks involved with this asset class.

Contents

Introduction

Family wealth is constantly under pressure: government fiscal policy that increases taxation; monetary policy that increases inflation; a growing number of descendants who have great expectations for their lifestyle; zero interest rate on bonds; volatile stock markets; high fees on private placements. High net-worth families must find a path through that landscape.

With each new generation, more people need to be supported by family wealth, but at the same time, fewer people know how to grow that wealth. Constant and conflicting pressures encourage wealth managers to stick with what they know, which is often rooted in the family business (even when younger generations are less in tune with its workings).

The unfortunate side effect of going with the tried and true is that as times change, it becomes less effective. Famously, Kodak had the first patents for the CMOS chip that empowered the digital camera revolution, but failed to see the value in the technology and chose to double-down on its film business: a strategic blunder that resulted in its eventual bankruptcy.[1]

I became an early investor in cryptocurrency because I noticed that all the smartest people I knew were running in the same direction. At a time when there was neither regulation nor a pool of knowledge about how the cryptocurrency industry worked, I both made and lost a lot of money really fast. I learned that investing in cryptocurrency had to be compatible with people's psychology.

At that time, the industry was much less sophisticated than it is now. There was a lot of mystery around what worked, so I had to become an expert in risk if I wanted to keep buying cryptocurrency. While trading in stocks and bonds, I had started building quantitative algorithms to develop risk and reward profiles for managing risk, and they turned out to get good results in cryptocurrency.

I also discovered the virtues of being deliberate, methodical and intentional in building a long-term investment strategy and keeping my course through the turbulence of the cryptocurrency world where many new products fail. Part of my impetus for writing this book is to share my knowledge so that family offices can become educated enough to manage their own risk. As the first-generation wealth creator in my family, I am asking myself as I write what my son will need to know.

Perhaps you are part of the older generation in your family office, under pressure from the youngsters to take advantage of the great gains to be made in emerging technologies that you may not understand. You might be savvy about traditional finance, but view the cryptocurrency industry as the Wild West (which, in some ways, it still is). This is the book your children need to buy for you.

Perhaps you belong to the younger or middle generation, seeking tactics to counter the typical fears that surface around cryptocurrency: "It's only for criminals"; "The government will ban it"; "It's not backed by anything". Then there are the current debates in the cryptocurrency space. What is the industry doing about quantum cryptography? What is it doing about energy consumption?

These are all legitimate concerns and there are reasons why the industry will generate its own solutions. Most fears and objections are at least partly rooted in reality, but they can all be managed. *Cryptocurrency Risk Management* will help you balance the risks to construct a suitable allocation.

The first part of the book will take you through how the cryptocurrency markets work and the decisions you need to make to build your portfolio, and show you why right now is a good time to invest in cryptocurrency. It will demonstrate the principles that will help you to make good capital deployment decisions: slow down; curate rather than collect investments;

don't be swayed by the next hot thing. In addition, it will talk you through how to choose your asset or type of cryptocurrency, the best investment strategies for what you want to achieve and how much of your portfolio to allocate to a given asset. These are the skills from traditional finance, adjusted for cryptocurrency conditions.

Many of the risks you will encounter will be familiar from traditional finance, but have a scary new dimension because cryptocurrencies are liquid assets, the markets are 24/7/365 and many new cryptocurrency projects can be short lived. The next big thing can vanish and take your money with it. While there can be astounding gains in speculating on new projects, the more likely outcome is astounding losses, because the success rate is so low. You need a solid system for selecting investable tokens that are likely to stay investable.

In addition, cryptocurrency transactions are immutable and cryptocurrencies are bearer assets: if someone tricks you into handing over your tokens, they get to keep them. There is little protection against fraud; in fact, some seemingly fraudulent activities such as market manipulation and insider trading are legal in cryptocurrency. There is also no bank involved to recall the funds if you inadvertently mistype a twenty-eight-digit address. You are dealing on cryptocurrency exchanges that have little regulation (although they have become much better quality and, in the US, capable of being System and Organization Controls (SOC) 2 compliant[2] and often insured up to a point).

For family wealth managers with transactions frequently in six, seven or eight figures, these are all serious concerns, but we do not need to be paralyzed by them. We can never truly eliminate a risk. Instead, we need to think in terms of whether we can mitigate the risk and what percentage of it can be mitigated.

After reading *Cryptocurrency Risk Management*, you will be much better informed about the emerging world you find yourself in and able to proceed with confidence. You will understand the areas where you most need to educate yourself and those in which you might need more technical sophistication, and you will be able to decide whether you want to build this sophistication internally, acquire it or hire it via the increasingly good-quality crypto funds.

The second part of *Cryptocurrency Risk Management* is your risks primer. You can use this any time as a quick reference for specific concerns, but reading the Part Two chapters in sequence will give you the big picture of the risk landscape.

Part Two will start with the class of risks that are already most reported in the news media and therefore most widely understood by the layperson: those relating to changes in market price. Then we will examine risks relating to governmental and regulatory factors. These require a long view as they might well change over the course of generations—family office managers are trying to future-proof wealth against an unknown regulatory landscape.

The next main group of risks contains those broadly classed as operational—the nature of holding and investing in cryptocurrency makes many of them inevitable. These are risks related to technology, cyber-security and counterparties, which we will examine in detail. Finally, we will look at the risks related to being human (in some ways, the hardest to manage).

It's a human impulse to feel left behind; to feel fear of missing out (FOMO); to want to be involved in what's hot. Remember, you are in an industry that generates huge wealth and if you are consistent, methodical and well informed (or can access the expertise you need), you can find a strategy that will bring rewards in the long term and does not need to be swayed by the headlines on the news.

You're on an exciting new path and this is your guidebook. If you're heading for the Wild West, make sure to take this guide, along with your natural skepticism and spirit of adventure.

PART ONE
HOW CRYPTOCURRENCY WORKS

The chapters in this part take you through the key decisions you need to make to build your cryptocurrency portfolio and help you create a system for deliberate intentional investing.

1
Avoiding The Family Wealth Death Spiral

Operating a family office is highly challenging. The wealth creator who establishes the office must design an organization that will work with today's laws and regulations as well as for future generations when the regulatory environment may be different. Not only does the office have to survive ever-changing financial markets, it must also survive the family's interpersonal relationships through marriage, divorce, births and deaths. Alongside all this, it must manage the family wealth in such a way that financial stability is ensured for many future generations.

Family office founders must navigate the tension between "governing from the grave," where the rules are rigid, versus allowing future generations the flexibility to adapt to the environment in which they find themselves. A common approach is to seek to equalize the allocations to family members in the pursuit of fairness, but this may come at the cost of the longevity of the family office as some inherit money before they are prepared to manage it well. Too frequently, the financial support runs out in two or three generations and family members end up at odds with one another.

Seeking safety through growth

The first impulse that most families have when designing their family office is: "I want to be safe. I want to invest our money safely so it will last for generations." That works well over one person's lifetime, but will not support a family that increases in size every few years.

When managing multi-generational wealth, the office becomes responsible for more than the immediate family. It is also responsible for future generations that will likely be far more numerous. It is common for a family of five members to grow to fifty to sixty members in just three generations, including wives, husbands and extended family. The blessings of a large family are many, but the family requires investment strategies to keep pace with its growth.

What often happens is that family members realize, after several years or decades or even generations of conservative investing, that the money will run out by generation three, four or five. They then decide they need to take on more risk in the hope of accelerating growth to keep up with the expanding family, the taxes that always seem to go up and other unforeseen pressures that emerge. For example, the scale of a family's operations might in itself make it a target for lawsuits, and just one lawsuit can wipe out enough wealth to present a serious setback. A big market drawdown (decline) can have a similar effect.

The family members may feel that they need to grow wealth urgently. They decide, "We're going to get involved in some better investments" or "We'll incorporate venture capital to gain exposure to start-ups" or "We'll invest in emerging asset classes" or "We'll invest in Chinese technology stocks." The impulse to grow the portfolio is correct, but growth comes at a cost.

It's rarely clear at the outset which growth stocks will outperform others and the downside risk can be tremendous. Tesla stock, which is an example of a high-risk investment that paid off, has ballooned and valuation is now part of the S&P 500 as of 2022, but as recently as 2019, Tesla was weeks away from bankruptcy.[3] Families that invested heavily in Tesla put their descendants' future at substantial risk.

The names of the high-growth firms that did not survive are lost to history. This is a typical case of survivorship bias, where investors only remember the firms that continue to exist.

SURVIVORSHIP BIAS

An example of survivorship bias in finance is when studies on a certain type of instrument or asset only use databases that contain data about those that currently exist in the market, and are therefore more resilient than those that have failed. Alternatively, studies on the profitability of certain industries might neglect to include financial information about companies that have closed for a variety of reasons, including bankruptcy, mergers and acquisitions or poor performance. By only basing evaluation on the most successful examples, analysts are drawing conclusions that are skewed positively and not reflecting real-life conditions.

The Corporate Finance Institute (CFI) showed in a study of mutual funds that including only those that were still active showed an average return of 9%.[4] When the CFI included funds that were eligible for the survey, but had closed, average return dropped to 3%. It can be hard for researchers to avoid survivorship bias, the CFI concluded, because the data they are using are also based on observations of "surviving" companies.

Family conflict

Managing family wealth is particularly challenging because there may be multiple viewpoints on how the role should be executed, with all contributors to the discussions needing to be heard and perceived as important. The natural hierarchy that exists within the family might not reflect the relative levels of skill and knowledge about managing investments.

There is the risk of loss of reputation for a family wealth manager who takes the apparently safe route of staying with tried-and-tested conservative investments (and is therefore blamed for failing to grow capital) or, conversely, makes an investment that ends in a large loss. There is also a risk of lawsuit: it is common for family members to sue one another over what they perceive as bad investments that one party has made, among other unfairness. Any pre-existing family conflicts, such as sibling rivalries or one family member being ostracized, are amplified when the need to protect family wealth is added into the mix.

The British TV drama *Downton Abbey*, set in the early 20th century, is the ultimate family wealth horror movie. The Earl of Grantham loses all his wife's family money speculating on railroad stocks, which were the tech stocks of the day. Once able to recapitalize through a dramatic family inheritance from his soon-to-be son-in-law, he is captivated by a new and exciting investment opportunity in the US with Charles Ponzi (the swindler who is credited with inventing the eponymous Ponzi Scheme).[5]

The knowledge deficit

A common cause of capital being depleted is families switching repeatedly between taking too little and too much risk: buying at the top of the market and selling at the bottom, when the opposite is more likely to be effective. To avoid this see-sawing pattern, a family needs a level of institutional knowledge of how to invest and what to invest in, which is often lacking. In addition, they need a well-thought-out investment strategy, which each successive generation understands and can adapt, so that they can remain confident in pursuing it over time.

Family offices that have supported three or more generations are likely to observe that successive generations become increasingly detached from the original family business. In the first generation of family wealth, there's often a business owner. Either they have sold a business or the business is the foundation for the family office. As the first-generation family office founder either built the business or was deeply involved with it, they have tacit knowledge of it. The second generation hears their stories, but the knowledge they receive is often indirect and prone to loss as years pass and memories fade.

By generation three, the stories are based on such distant memories, they lose practical application detail and seem less than relevant. Also, the family business, which was so prosperous a few generations prior, is now operating in an environment completely different than the one in which it was founded. Generation-three family office inheritors often receive criticism for failing the family business, but it is equally true that the world changes over the course of between 60 and 100 years and the ideas that made the business successful at the outset may not work as well in the new environment.

As a result, not only is the business failing, but the family has not developed its investment thesis, so there can be a knowledge and experience gap when it comes to investing in higher growth assets. If two generations have been conservative, focused on capital preservation, how can generation three or four learn to perform due diligence on venture capital start-up investments? How will they know how much to allocate to Chinese technology stocks or cryptocurrencies?

A typical pattern is a wealthy parent gives their son or daughter money to invest in the hopes of helping them develop the skills to manage money, but the investment fails. The scarce resource here is not money, but knowledge and experience, without which it is impossible to tell which investments will be successful.

Another common scenario is where a family has a large lump sum to invest from an inheritance, sale of a business or winning the lottery. The family members do not have the expertise to manage the money themselves, so they rely on investment managers. The fees are high and the family has a lot of eggs in one basket.

Investors often underestimate the difference between managing a small portfolio that is accumulated over many years versus investing lump sums after a windfall. The two scenarios require different strategies because the capital is being deployed in large portions at one point in time versus in many small portions over a long period. Selecting investments that will not expose the portfolio to significant risk of losing the family's windfall takes far more knowledge and experience than, for example, dollar-cost averaging into an index fund portfolio over decades. Dollar-cost averaging means that an investor purchases similar amounts of stocks over a period of years, so some are purchased during low markets and some are purchased during high markets. The net effect is that the investor builds a portfolio of securities at neither the lowest or highest price, but at a good price.

The gap is exacerbated by the tendency for investors to focus on the knowledge that has been true during their lifetimes. The problem is that these cycles can be long. The debt cycle is about eighty years; the stock market cycle is between ten and twenty years, so investors under seventy years old who are relying on their own experience are at a distinct disadvantage: they will not be seeing the whole picture.

HISTORY TRUMPS LIVED EXPERIENCE

The eminent hedge fund manager Ray Dalio said that early in his career, he had to become a historian because he was running into problems in the economy that had happened before, but not in his lifetime.[6] In 1998, I achieved my first professional job during my sophomore year of college working as a systems manager at the university I was attending. One of the perks of becoming a full-time employee and part-time student was that I was able to contribute to a 403(b) retirement plan with an employer match. Unfortunately, that was the worst time to start investing as the tech bubble popped and crashed the stock market throughout 2000 and 2001.

Fast forward to 2006, when I had a better job making more money and was able to make the maximum tax-deferred retirement contribution for the first time. Then came the Global Financial Crisis of 2008 where the market crashed again and did not recover net of inflation until 2016. My lived experience taught me that markets trade in a range over a cycle that lasts about ten to twelve years.

Today, through my research in stock-market history, I know that my early experiences were somewhat unusual. We can consider ourselves lucky that we have the benefit of thousands of years of recorded history at our fingertips.

If we restrict ourselves to our direct experiences, our sample size is too small because we humans are limited in our lifespans. Parents who attempt to convince their children of the wisdom of their strategies are often performing a disservice to their descendants.

My grandfather lived during the Carter administration, when interest rates were 10% plus and he could buy a certificate of deposit (CD) that was guaranteed by a bank and yielded 8–12% for thirty years. If I'd invested in CDs during my lifetime, I'd be impoverished because inflation has been higher than the CD rates.

Families must seek balance between extracting the knowledge of previous generations and adapting to the future. My grandfather's generation could never have imagined something like a cryptocurrency because they did not have computers during their working life. Today, I'm a first-generation family wealth creator focused on how to manage a cryptocurrency portfolio (the opportunity of my day) with the context that my son's portfolio will likely be as different from mine as mine is from my grandfather's.

Slow down

To preserve and grow family wealth, portfolio managers must slow down to the point that it feels almost painful. Everyone's first instinct is to make changes quickly, but the cost of mistakes can be devastating. While inflation is an ever-present force in the financial markets, the 3% standard rate of inflation is easily outweighed by the possibility of a 50% or more loss from a poor investment decision. During the interim, portfolio managers can deploy excess liquidity to a simple portfolio of treasury bonds or perhaps treasury inflation-protected securities (TIPS) to avoid the possibility of loss from a bank failure.

A manager needs to steer a multi-generational portfolio more like a barge than a race car. They should nudge it gently, partly because the family members have deep expertise in the existing portfolio, partly because people need time to adapt to new ideas. Knowing this, family wealth managers can proactively make incremental adaptations continuously so they do not need to make drastic changes in the future.

By slowing down, the family portfolio manager creates an opportunity to develop a comprehensive plan for the future asset allocation and the skills to manage the future portfolio, along with the time to incrementally phase the new allocation into the portfolio systematically.

Many investors are hostage to their deal flow. Perhaps they have a friend who is launching a technology start-up, so they invest in that; then a real-estate fund is pitched at a nice wine tasting, so they invest in that too; then they invest in an alternative energy fund during tax season in an attempt to reduce their tax liability. Then the capital calls come in and they have lost track of all the commitments they made to the various funds. They often don't even remember why they invested in the first place.

Family wealth managers need to be gardeners, not gatherers. Imagine the difference between planting a garden versus collecting acorns in the forest. Gardening takes more preparation, more knowledge, more patience, more skills; but it is also far more productive.

By starting with a sober, well-thought-out plan and being deliberate, intentional and methodical, a wealth manager ensures the family gains not only investment returns, but also peace of mind. This is another good reason to slow down.

Indexing and today's investors

The Modern Portfolio Theory that most wealth advisors and money managers use today is based on the work of economist Henry Markowitz in the 1970s.[7] Markowitz discovered that he could create portfolios that had high returns and low risk by combining asset classes. This led to the idea of stock and bond portfolios (for example 70% stocks, 30% bonds) in which portfolio managers pair assets to create better returns for the risk they're taking. Because bonds are often inversely correlated to stocks and equities are strongly correlated to the general stock market, an investor can calculate an appropriate ratio.

Investors and advisors tend to over-depend on Modern Portfolio Theory, like many good heuristics, but by reading Markowitz thoroughly and re-calculating his theories with the metrics from today's economy, we get far different conclusions than in his day. This is because much of the math that Markowitz performed does not work when bond yields are zero or near-zero. His work was developed during an era where bond yields were approximately 6% and stock returns were around 8%. His premise was: if you concede a small amount of return on the upside, the risk premia, you receive a benefit in terms of capital preservation.

WHAT IS AN EFFICIENT FRONTIER?

An efficient frontier is a technique derived from Markowitz's work, where all possible portfolios are compared. For example, a 1% stocks, 99% bonds portfolio; then a 2% stocks, 98% bonds portfolio; all the way up to a 99% stocks, 1% bonds portfolio. Then these values are plotted on a chart, which creates a curve that usually looks like a spear. The optimal allocation— the one that is exactly at the tip of the spear—has the maximum return for the amount of risk taken.

Markowitz's theory is sound and it has helped a lot of people, but it has limitations. It is especially useful for investors who are dollar averaging into the market over forty years by saving small amounts each year during their working life, but it is less useful where family wealth portfolio managers are tasked with deploying large windfalls periodically. It is a different type of problem when an investor needs to deploy $50 million after a liquidity event, for example, and still be able to sleep at night.

Investing is as much a psychological exercise as it is mathematical. Many investors are wedded to index funds, largely because John C. (Jack) Bogle, founder of the Vanguard Financial Group, authored a number of popular books that have developed a cult of followers who call themselves Bogleheads.[8] These Bogleheads periodically gather for festivals of frugality, their core premise being that actively managed funds don't beat the stock market.

In one sense, they are correct: it is rare for actively managed funds to beat index funds in terms of average arithmetic return. However, many actively managed funds are seeking to provide similar upside to the index, but at a reduced risk. The Boglehead community ignores the risk side of the equation and judges actively managed funds by a standard the funds do not seek to achieve.

The trouble with arithmetic returns is that they do not account for losses very well. For example, starting with a balance of $1million:

Year	Annual Return	End Balance
1	8%	$1,080,000.00
2	10%	$1,188,000.00
3	-50%	$594,000.00
4	50%	$891,000.00
Total Return		-$109,000.00

Arithmetic Mean	4.5%
Actual Return	-10.9% or -2.7% per year
CAGR	-2.4% per year

The flaw in the Bogleheads' argument is that arithmetic returns are not symmetric (as logarithmic returns are), so a better metric for comparison is compound annual growth rate (CAGR).[9] With an arithmetic return calculation, the average return of an investment that loses 100% of its value in year one and gains 200% of its value in year two has an average return of 50% per year, but the investor would still have $0.00 in their investment account.

Let's look at the S&P 500 with this knowledge in hand. Risk-return profile: 6–8% per year; 50–80% declines approximately once per decade; 10, 20 and 30% decline four or five times per decade.[10] If an actively managed fund can successfully avoid a substantial fraction of those down markets and participate in the majority of the S&P 500's return, its investors would find their equity balances far higher than those of the index investors.

Summary

Every investment comes at a cost, whether it's the soft cost of the time an investor spends performing due diligence, the opportunity cost of other investments or the hard cost of losing money if the investment does not pan out.

By slowing down, portfolio managers have an opportunity to build a comprehensive strategy that is most likely to generate sufficient rewards for the cost. They can ask:

- What asset classes will we invest in and why?

- Does real estate have a role to play?

- What is the role of public equities?

- Does a bond allocation make sense with today's interest rates?

- How will we meet our short-term liquidity needs?

- How large a decline can the investors tolerate?

- What will be our withdrawal rate? How will that change if the market crashes?

- How can we balance our investment returns with taxation?

- What advisors do we need?

- How much correlation can we tolerate?

- How does a private equity investment affect our portfolio?

Regarding all new investments, the portfolio manager must ask:

- What are the returns?

- What are the risks?

- How is it taxed?

- What are the fees?

- What is the correlation to other assets in the portfolio?

There is no good reason to build a portfolio with multiple investments that are strongly linked to interest rates. While in theory the portfolio is diversified, its strong correlation to a single economic factor provides little improvement to risk. When a family creates a portfolio of this type, eventually the correlation will lead to large losses in down markets. Then the family will be reminded that investing is more than a mathematical exercise; it is deeply personal and psychological. Instead of using the down market as a rebalancing opportunity to accumulate assets at a great price, they tend to panic-sell and lock in losses instead of sticking to their plan.

It is preferable to pick three to five different asset classes that are not strongly correlated. Then the objective becomes to find the best opportunities for each category that you want for each asset class you want to invest in and to determine how much capital to allocate to each. We will look in more detail at diversifying by asset class in Chapter 4.

The solution to seesawing between overly aggressive and overly conservative portfolios is for a wealth manager to improve their understanding of risk and manage all its dimensions so the family can participate in high-growth assets with confidence.

2
Why Crypto For Family Wealth?

Family wealth, almost by definition, is conventional. It's nearly always rooted in aged industries that either have stopped growing or are growing less as generations go by, to the point where they are not likely to provide the growth needed to sustain the wealth.

If the family wealth is in oil and gas, for example, there is little uncertainty about the future of the investments. Every single pocket of oil and gas on the planet has been mapped; there is no more being discovered and we know what oil and gas is worth based upon the market price on any given week. There is, therefore, little chance of a 10x return on oil and gas investments because all investors have the same information. Similarly, in real estate, return on investment is predictable and the potential for growth is limited without the investor adding value through their knowledge and hard work.

Making space in a portfolio for emerging technologies allows you as portfolio manager the opportunity to create the level of growth a family needs. That does not mean completely selling out of your old industries, but gaining exposure and expertise in whatever the technologies of the future will be, for example robotics, blockchain or private space travel.

Cryptocurrency is one of the most prominent catalysts for growth due to its asymmetric growth.

ASYMMETRIC GROWTH

Asymmetric growth occurs when an investment is undertaken where the potential gain is much higher than the potential loss. These types of investments are desirable, but rare.

For example, when buying an equity (stock), the full cost of the position must be paid and the potential risk is 100% of the position if the business fails. By contrast, a call options contract, the position is opened for a small fee (less than 5% of the cost to buy the equity), which is the maximum loss of the position, but the potential upside is unlimited. The downside is constrained, but the upside is unconstrained.

It is important to look for asymmetries in investing when pursuing portfolio growth because a series of small risks can reap outsized rewards.

The rate of return of the cryptocurrency market is nearly 100% per year, whereas the yields on an oil well might be 2%–4% and the capitalization rate on real estate would typically be 3%–5%. The rate of return on equity index funds over the long term is 6%–8%. With the returns on emerging technologies being so much higher, it doesn't take much exposure to them in a portfolio to catalyze the growth you need: between 3% and 5% of portfolio exposure to digital assets can provide substantial lift to portfolio total return with limited downside.

The next internet

The best comparison to the arrival of cryptocurrency is the point when the internet emerged. The internet was a new technology that enabled a succession of other technologies. We are still not at the end of the internet's influence and cannot determine what it might create in the future.

Just as we don't know yet exactly which companies will succeed on the internet, we certainly don't know which assets will thrive in the cryptocurrency world. What we do know is that there's tremendous potential and an opportunity to participate in the growth of this emerging industry, and that's a thrilling and usually profitable place to be.

There's infinitely more money to be made by investing in, working in or otherwise focusing on industries that are emerging rather than those that are established. This isn't a recent trend; it is not limited to the modern sense in terms of computers and software. This has been true since humans learned how to use fire.

The first person to use fire had a huge advantage over everyone who didn't. The first person who had steel had a huge advantage over someone who only had iron, whether for weaponry or commercial applications. You can draw a line through human progress and see that it has tracked with technological improvement. When a piece of technology emerges that makes something new possible, society blossoms around it. Our job as entrepreneurs and investors is to unlock the possibilities of those crucial catalyst-for-change technologies.

Cryptocurrency is exciting because we're seeing in real time myriad technologies developing as a result. It used to be that cryptocurrency just meant Bitcoin, but now Ethereum has emerged as a solid number two asset with smart contracts.[11] The Ethereum smart contract platform spawned thousands of new projects, enabling decentralized finance (DeFi), a whole new segment of the cryptocurrency industry.

Now, there are non-fungible tokens (NFTs) where blockchain and smart contracts are used to assign ownership to digital intellectual property. What comes next? We really don't know, but we do know that this is something new, and new industries often create fortunes.

A family office investor seeking high-growth assets in their portfolio, maybe because wealth managers have been too conservative in the past, will find cryptocurrency is a good option to explore. What are the key things the investor needs to know?

As people learn about cryptocurrency, they progress through three levels of understanding. The first level is focused on the idea of "magic internet money." Tim Berners-Lee, Director of the W3C, which sponsors the W3C Web Payments Working Group,[12] said, "The blockchain and the web will connect together in lots of interesting ways"[13] foretelling the emergence of Web 3.0.

With the emergence of cryptocurrencies applying the blockchain technology, the internet now has its own payments mechanism not tied to the traditional financial system. The immediate appeal to someone new to cryptocurrency might be: "Wow, this allows people to send money without a bank twenty-four hours per day and seven days per week with minimal fees, and I can see the transaction clear in real time." Without Bitcoin or one of the other crypto platforms, we wouldn't have a mechanism to do that. If we didn't want to use a bank, we would have to send paper currency or a gold bar, which doesn't scale well across geography or for large payments.

The second level of understanding is along the lines of: "The underlying blockchain technology is powerful. Look at all the potential of an immutable consensus-driven blockchain. This technology will enable new industries. We could tokenize art and real estate titles, potentially even voting." At this level of understanding, the focus is on possibilities enabled by blockchain algorithms that power the cryptocurrency and smart contract platforms, and the intuition is that everything needs to be on the blockchain.

Once we understand the potential of blockchain, there is an impulse to seek out the "best blockchain." This investigation sometimes leads investors towards projects that might be focused on an intriguing or enticing piece of technology, but don't have a long track record, so are not investable from a portfolio allocation perspective. This second level of understanding is still not deep enough.

The third and highest level of understanding is about the value of the cryptocurrency blockchains and their relative resilience against attack. Like the internet, the cryptocurrency network derives its value from the large numbers of people using it. Metcalfe's Law states that the value of the network grows exponentially as nodes are added to it: a network effect.[14]

We can compare this phenomenon with the growth of the telephone system in the final decades of the 19th century into the 20th. At first, it was a novelty for wealthy people who could call a few of their wealthy friends. Once the telephone became ubiquitous, a tremendous amount of commerce and new technologies flowed from and were enabled by this one network. We can attribute all the value that was created by the telephone network to the increasing number of people attached to it.

The same principle holds true in the cryptocurrency networks. As more people use them, they become more robust and resilient against attacks. The larger the cryptocurrency network, the safer it becomes and the more confident people feel in using it.

The more participants there are on the network, the less likelihood there is of a 51% attack (where someone owns more than 50% of the staking or hashing power of a cryptocurrency network, so can change its rules). In smaller networks, this type of attack is common. A wealthy individual can control enough cryptocurrency miners (the specialized computers used for mining Bitcoin and other digital assets) or nodes to attack a network, change the rules, take all the coins and sell them or otherwise negatively affect the integrity of the network. This sort of attack is not possible against mature networks such as Bitcoin or Ethereum, which are resilient not only against individual or corporate-level attacks, but state-level attacks where a government might try to commandeer the network, because their hashing power collectively would be the largest supercomputer in existence.

PROOF OF WORK AND PROOF OF STAKE

There are two main competing consensus models for how blocks are added to a blockchain: proof of work and proof of stake. Proof of work is the model favored by Bitcoin, where cryptocurrency miners use immense processing power and electrical energy to solve complicated cryptographic puzzles in exchange for a reward if they are correct.[15]

Proof of stake is the consensus mechanism Ethereum is moving toward, where owners of the asset stake their tokens using specialized software to become a validator.[16] These validators are responsible for deciding which blocks are added to the network and in which order.

These consensus mechanisms are important for the health and functioning of the cryptocurrency network. If one participant is able to gain control of the network, they could change the rules, which would allow them to steal money, mint new tokens or otherwise harm the investor community.

Why crypto now?

One of the biggest long-standing arguments in favor of cryptocurrency is that it's an asset that cannot be manipulated by the government. In the case of Bitcoin, there is a slight amount of inflation, but it's declining over time. This generally means that the monetary supply of government-backed currencies, such as the dollar or the pound or any of the major world currencies, is increasing much faster than the supply of Bitcoin.

Cryptocurrencies are outside governments' jurisdiction, so no government can print more Bitcoin. The supply of Bitcoin is fixed; there will only ever be 21 million Bitcoins. Over time, those coins will be released slowly, and the general intuition is that they will be scarce and therefore valuable, as long as there's increased adoption. This contrasts with the central bank currencies that are being created, sometimes seemingly out of thin air, when governments need to fund a project or seek to influence public opinion.

Another factor in cryptocurrencies' favor is that we have had aggressive global monetary stimuli since 2000–2001 when the dot-com bubble burst. The US Federal Reserve has continued to cut interest rates and the rest of the world has largely followed. In 2008, interest rates were decreased to effectively zero, but even that wasn't sufficient to stimulate the economy.

In addition to a zero interest-rate policy (ZIRP), the Federal Reserve began a program of quantitative easing where it purchased assets, mostly mortgage-backed securities, to further stimulate the economy. In 2020–2021 during the COVID pandemic, the Federal Reserve repeated the ZIRP, began an asset purchase program and injected capital through direct (transfer payments) stimulus to individuals and businesses.

Many investors believe that Bitcoin will increase in value because fiat currencies, measured by the M2 money supply for the US dollar, will lose value more quickly than Bitcoin. M2 is "a measure of the US money stock that includes M1 (currency and coins held by the non-bank public, checkable deposits, and travelers' checks) plus savings deposits (including money market deposit accounts), small time deposits under $100,000, and shares in retail money market mutual funds."[17] The US dollar's M2 supply grows according to an exponential curve, while the supply of Bitcoin has a slowing supply. Despite tremendous volatility, the thesis that cryptocurrencies will lose their value less quickly than fiat currencies is sound over a long-enough time horizon.

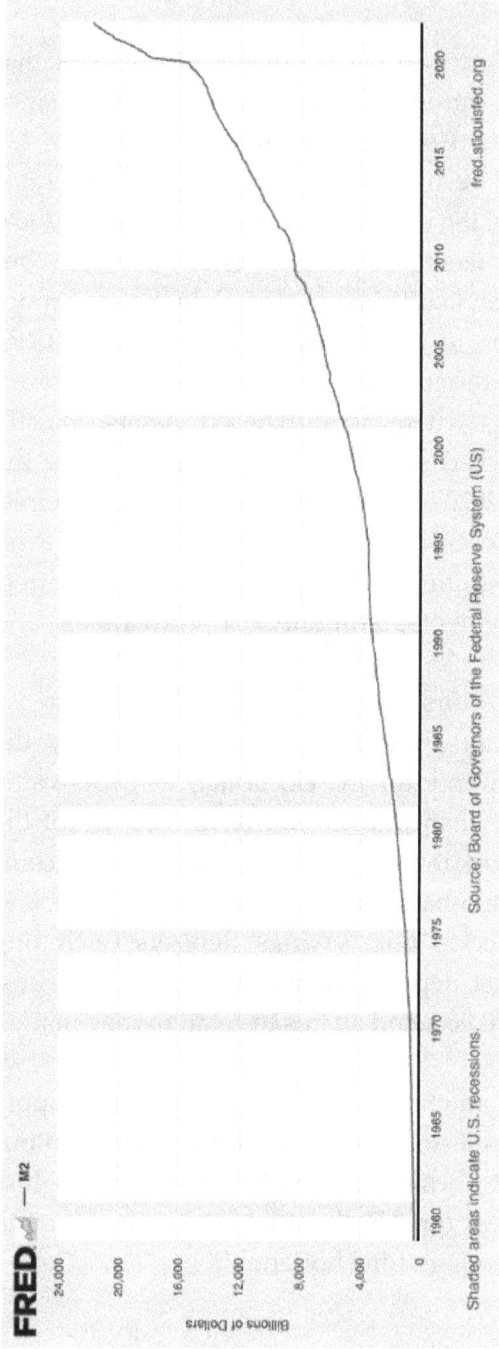

M2 [M2SL][18]

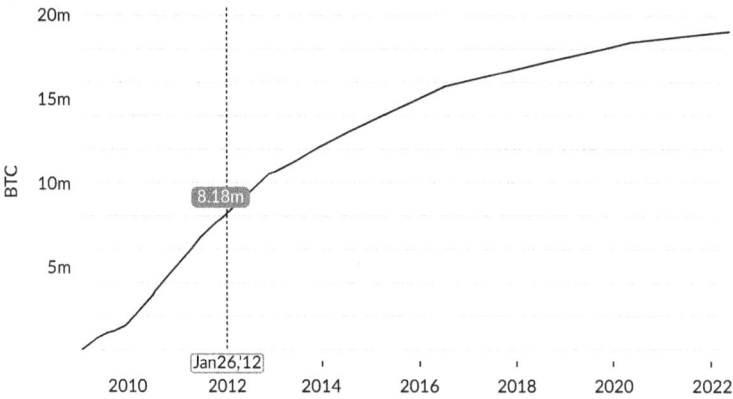

Total circulating Bitcoin: the total number of mined bitcoin that are currently circulating on the network [19]

In addition, cryptocurrencies as technological innovations are following the technology adoption curve. Pew Research notes that only 16% of Americans have invested in, traded or used cryptocurrency, which would put the technology at the mid stage of the early adopter phase of Rogers' Diffusion of Innovation model.[20]

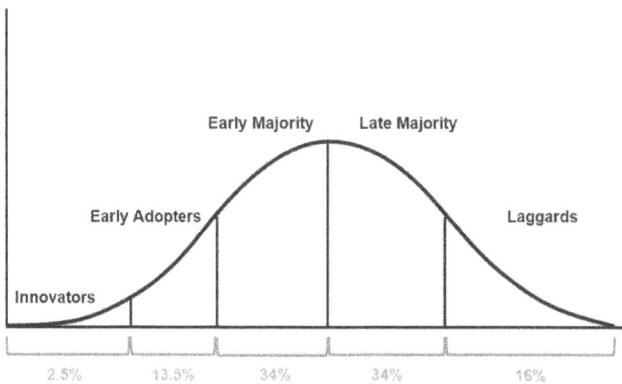

Diffusion of innovation[21]

The post-COVID era is challenging for monetary policy. In 2022, inflation rose to nearly 10% per year, while treasury yields remain low at around 3% yield.[22] Inflation has not been this high since the 1980s when the Federal Reserve, led by Paul Volcker, raised interest rates to over 15% during the Carter administration.

One difference between the US in 2022 and in 1980 is that the debt to gross domestic product (GDP) ratio was much lower in the 1980s at around 30%. In contrast, the debt in 2022 is over 120% of GDP. This high level of debt makes it challenging for the Federal Reserve to increase interest rates because the US government will need to pay this increased interest rate on their debt, which could cause further defaults on the government's obligations.

The idea that the US government could default on its obligations is controversial, but it has happened multiple times in the past. In 1933, President Franklin D. Roosevelt suspended the gold standard and devalued the US dollar in an attempt to stimulate the economy and increase exports.[23] In 1971, President Richard Nixon suspended all redemptions of the US dollar for gold, thus eliminating the gold standard.[24]

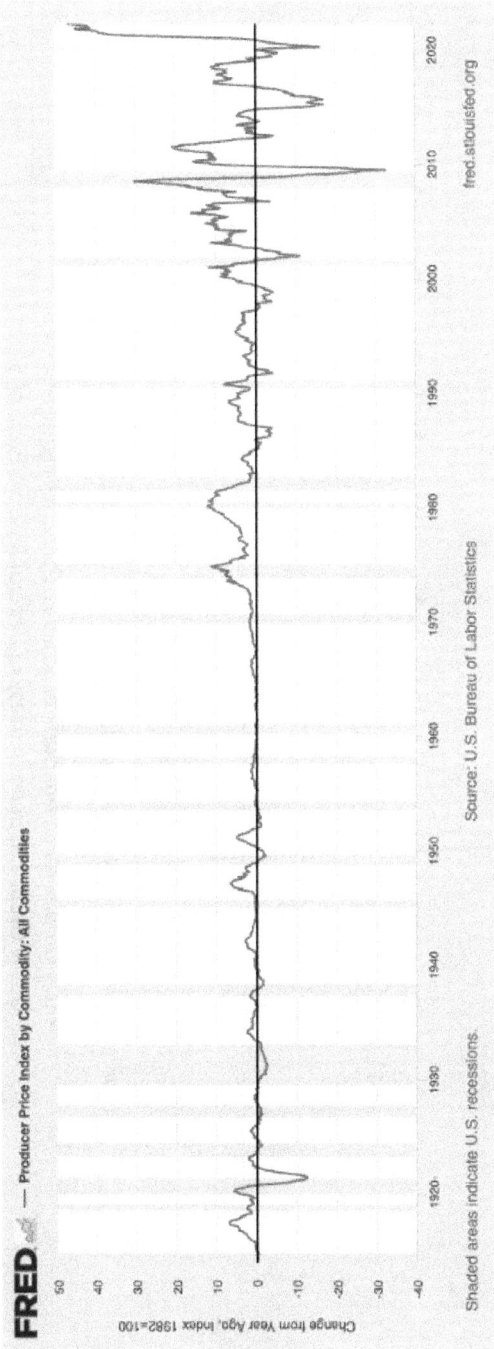

Producer price index by commodity: all commodities[25]

RED, FRED® Graphs ©Federal Bank of St Louis. 2022.
All rights reserved. All FRED® Graphs appear courtesy of Federal Reserve Bank of St Louis.

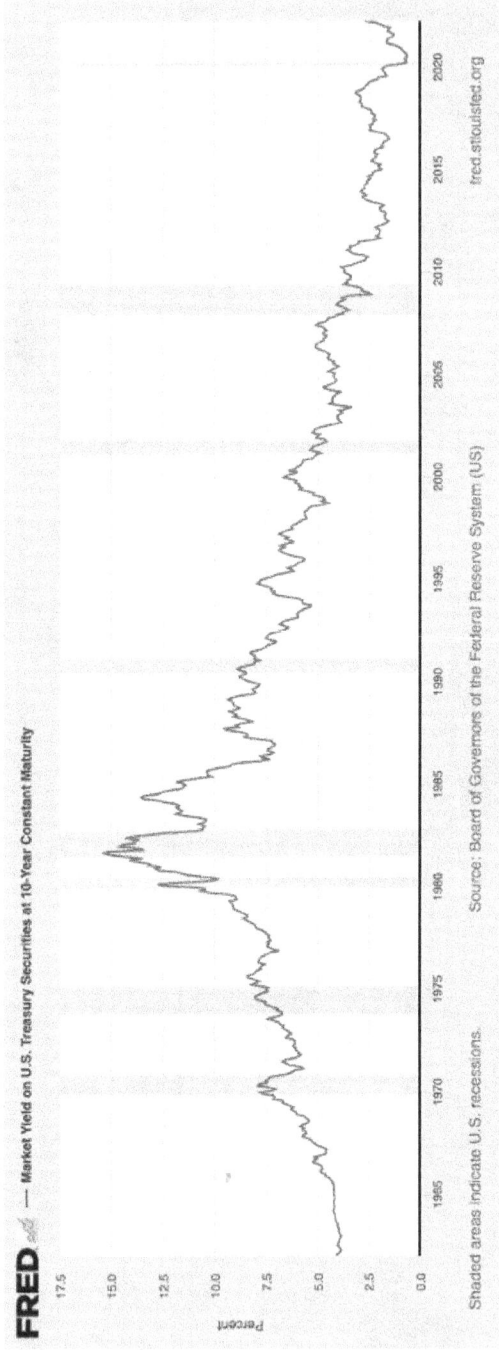

Market Yield on US Treasury Securities at 10-Year Constant Maturity [DGS10][26]

FRED® Graphs ©Federal Bank of St Louis. 2022. All rights reserved.
All FRED® Graphs appear courtesy of Federal Reserve Bank of St Louis.

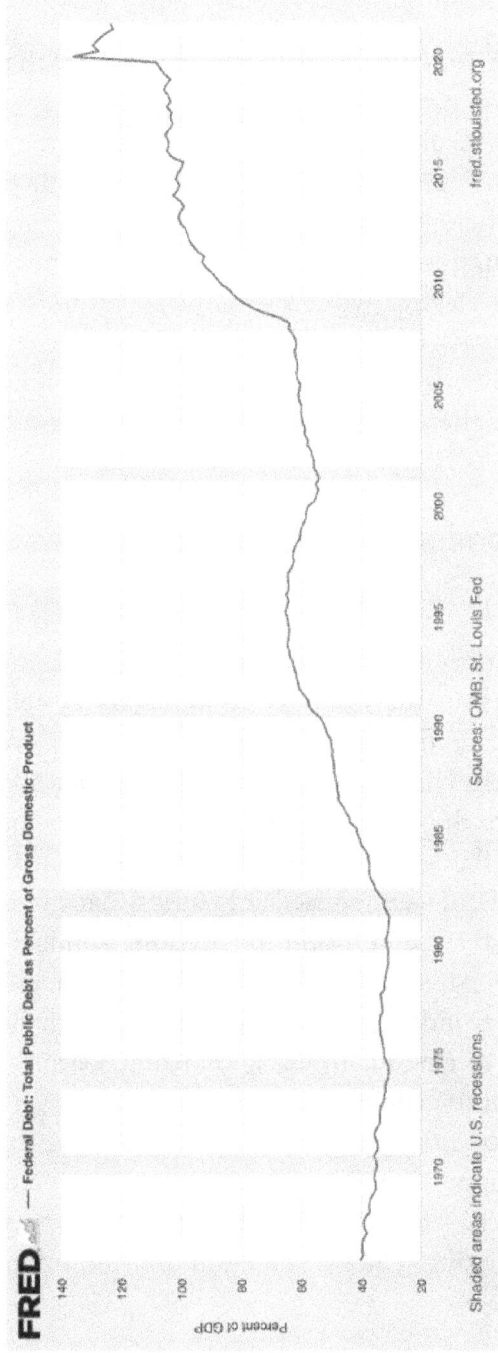

Federal debt: total public debt as percent of gross domestic product [27]

FRED® Graphs ©Federal Bank of St Louis. 2022. All rights reserved.
All FRED® Graphs appear courtesy of Federal Reserve Bank of St Louis.

In 2022, we entered an era that feels like another chaotic moment in world history. At the time of writing, the US is potentially at war with Russia over Ukraine and there's increased fear of nuclear engagements in the world. There are emerging threats from China, which is arming itself. Monetary policy is becoming less and less effective worldwide, and governments are acting in ways that citizens frequently feel are not in their best interests. For any investor, these are perilous times and there is no way to predict the outcome.

The blossoming cryptocurrency ecosystem

Many investors, especially younger investors, are intuitively distrustful of the entire monetary system and say it's time to build a new system. They believe the new system will look more like Bitcoin, Tesla and SpaceX where the industries of the future are being invented. In the same way Tesla disrupted General Motors and Ford—entrenched industries that many people thought could never be exciting—innovators like Elon Musk have disrupted the automobile industry. Every industry is being reimagined with the combination of cloud computing, machine learning, robotics and artificial intelligence.

The finance industry is no exception. The biggest change is happening in the cryptocurrency space, where internet users and computer programmers have disrupted banking. Once a powerful and important institution, banks have become unnecessary for many of their core functions (storing currency, transferring money, tracking currency ownership). The other features a bank provides are rapidly being developed by a cohort of start-up companies that seek to make the existing financial system obsolete. The cryptocurrency ecosystem is blossoming so that it can stand alone as well as integrate with the existing financial system.

There's even an increased push by central banks to start using cryptocurrencies due to the technological advantages of digital assets. Many countries don't want to use Bitcoin because the value is unstable and they cannot control it; instead, they want to create a central bank digital currency (CBDC).

It's easy to see why a CBDC would be appealing. During the 2020 pandemic, governments needed to deliver a lot of stimuli to the economy very quickly. The US federal government (and most countries used a similar system) distributed money to employers with the idea that they would keep their employees in work and, if employees continued to receive an income, the economy would not go into an immediate depression.

In the aftermath, we've found out many of the employers took the money and invested it in stocks and bonds and investment assets, so the funds weren't given to the employees and used to stimulate the economy. With a CBDC if a government wanted to deliver a stimulus, they could deliver it directly to the people, into their wallets. This is usually more effective as a stimulus because employees who find extra money in their account tend to spend it rather than invest it.

In 2013, when I started accumulating Bitcoin at a price of $20.00, I made the purchase on a website, drove across town and sent $500 per day to a stranger on the internet. Not only was there a risk that they would not send the coins, but the process was cumbersome even for small investments.

With all this complexity, I was less than diligent about going to the trouble of making the purchases. Those who stuck with it or found other ways to acquire the tokens have made vast sums. Unfortunately, many of the early Bitcoin holders did not recognize its value and lost their funds due to computer hard-drive crashes, missing backups or theft. Also, the liquidity of the market was poor; even if I'd had the patience to accumulate large sums of Bitcoin, it would have been equally painful to sell them at that time.

The cryptocurrency industry is now more mature and good-quality firms such as cryptocurrency exchanges are common. The US has a futures market for Bitcoin with one for Ethereum expected soon. Exchange traded funds (ETFs) and other exchange traded products are emerging around the world. There are publicly traded trusts to gain exposure to Bitcoin and other cryptocurrencies, and increasingly there are publicly traded equities for firms specializing in cryptocurrency.

Cryptocurrency institutions have improved rapidly, in particular because the industry has recognized the financial value of Bitcoin and other cryptocurrencies. Now consumers are demanding that this financial value is insured.

Years ago, cryptocurrency exchanges were not insurable because the processes, procedures and best practices to manage them were not agreed upon. This resulted in catastrophe in 2014 when Mt. Gox, an extremely popular early cryptocurrency exchange, became insolvent. Even today it remains unclear as to whether the failure of Mt. Gox was due to incompetence, theft or fraud.

Today, many firms have achieved SOC 2 compliance: a set of policies and procedures that are agreed upon as the best in class. To become insurable, cryptocurrency exchanges must go through an SOC 2 audit that helps them look for unmitigated risks. The auditor assesses the exchange's policies, procedures, cybersecurity, client interface and internal governance, and verifies that there is sufficient oversight when monies are being transferred. Therefore, many of today's cryptocurrency exchanges are insured in a meaningful way against loss, theft and fraud, and all of the actors along that process are also insured.

It's common for institutions that want to hold a large amount of cryptocurrency to use a third-party custodian service that's separate from their cryptocurrency exchange because it's easier to let a specialist handle that complexity rather than build it in-house. Asset managers such as hedge funds and venture capital firms are increasingly building the capability to manage cryptocurrency portfolios as they see rising demand from their clients. We are seeing the emergence of a web of industries that have reached a high level of maturity in terms of risk.

Many years ago, this process happened with equities. At one time, if an investor bought a share of the Shell Oil Company stock, they received a paper stock certificate. In the earliest days, stockbrokers would meet purchasers at a coffee house to sell the issue. This was not secure because the stock certificates could be stolen or damaged.

Over time, the traditional financial system developed high-quality industries to solve the system's problems. There are now clearing houses, transfer agents and custodians who say who owns what, while electronic brokerages track and manage the client trading activity.

All these layers are being replicated rapidly in the cryptocurrency industry where they are held to the same standard as the firms in the traditional financial system. There is a tremendous effort occurring behind the scenes to protect investors and legitimize the industry.

As with any investment, the more educated you can be, the more you can protect yourself.

Bridging the family gap

The previous chapter touched on the tension between generations in family offices. One of the common tensions that emerges is that the younger generations don't feel heard. They don't feel that what they're interested in matters; that there's a place for them.

Cryptocurrency offers a fantastic opportunity to develop the next generation of family office participants by drawing them into territory that they find interesting and exciting. Emerging technology gives the younger generations something they can make their own. They don't tend to want to be involved in real estate or oil and gas; they want to be involved in electric vehicles, solar and private space exploration. They don't want to be Forex traders and trade the old currencies; they want to trade cryptocurrencies where if they're right, it matters.

By building expertise in this area, the younger generations can contribute their passion and expertise to help the family create an allocation to cryptocurrency. This fulfills a family office's fiduciary responsibility while bringing in some much-needed growth, and the excitement that this sparks in the younger generations helps them feel involved in the family concerns.

Summary

Now is the time to invest in cryptocurrency, as the industry has matured enough for solutions to early problems to evolve and the standards of the traditional financial sector become more easily replicated. Alongside this, cryptocurrency remains an exciting and disruptive field with enormous growth potential that the next generation of family office managers is well placed to enjoy.

Alongside the thrills of emerging technology, of course, sits a healthy measure of fear of the unknown. This will be the focus of the next chapter.

3

Crypto Fears And How To Manage Them

In any emerging technology, there are things to learn. By definition, a family office is entering new territory by investing in cryptocurrency. The ideas that apply to traditional stocks and bond investing, for example, may not apply here. It is a new generation of technology, so we need to define what the threats to it are, along with the risks and rewards involved.

In this chapter, we will examine the common fears and questions that come up when family offices consider investing in cryptocurrency. We will discover that most of these fears are rooted in an element of truth and the risks are legitimate, but there are technologies and products emerging to address them (the second part of this book considers the mitigation of common risks in more detail).

These are the most common and widespread concerns and beliefs.

Quantum computers will break the blockchain

It is true that quantum computing does pose a risk to cryptocurrencies because most utilize public key cryptography algorithms, especially elliptic curve digital signature algorithm (ECDSA). These algorithms make a message computationally inexpensive to encrypt, but expensive to decrypt.

To encipher the transaction effectively involves multiplying two large numbers (called a key), which is simple for a computer to perform. To discover the two numbers that were multiplied is more difficult than multiplying them. This makes decrypting the message more difficult than encrypting it, so much so that it would take all the computing power on the Earth approximately 460 million years to decrypt a message of the size common for Bitcoin. At present, that's a difficult enough algorithm to provide security.

However, quantum computers have the potential to be better at solving these types of problems than traditional computers are at creating them. After a classical computer encrypts a message, a quantum computer may be able to decrypt it much faster than classic computers would. That means that maybe, it could be cracked in a timely and cost-effective manner.

There is some legitimate concern about this, but a more nuanced perspective is:

- Quantum computers would still have to be about 102,000 times more powerful than they are today to start breaking cryptocurrency transactions, so there is time to solve the problem.

- If a quantum computer can break Bitcoin, which uses strong cryptography and frequently has better security than most banks, this is a pervasive societal problem on a scale similar to the Y2K. We as a society will be highly incentivized to solve it as no secure communication will be possible for financial transactions, for example, or military order transmissions.

- Over time, if an attacker has access to an enormous quantum computer to do the decrypting, small quantum computers will become inexpensive, so they can be used for the encrypting. This may require the creation of new methods of quantum cryptography, but the incentives to do so will be high, and there will not be only one quantum computer; there will be many. Everyone will be on the same technology curve; it won't be the case that the attackers of blockchain will have quantum technology and the constructive users will not. There will always be people who want to defend the network because they have a financial incentive to make sure that it functions properly, is legitimized and is high quality.

It is true that small low-market-capitalization projects may not be able to adapt. As we considered in the last chapter, the networks may not be robust enough from a hash-rate perspective to maintain integrity. In other words, they may not have enough participants or developers to defend their network, so they could become prone to attack. For higher-quality projects that have a wide array of participants, that fear is overblown because it will be a pervasive problem for all of cryptography.

We as a society are incentivized to have good cryptography for electronic communication and there's an example of this that already exists today. As much of the cryptography that we're performing on traditional computers is computationally expensive and complex, it is really slow to run on a general purpose processor, which becomes a problem for secure websites whose speed is negatively impacted by the computational needs of the secure sockets layer (SSL) protocol. Many manufacturers have created a hardware chip for the servers that enables them to perform specific cryptography computations faster, so we have a precedent for creating new products that help solve our problems and make strong cryptography the norm.

Technologists and cryptographers have tools to address the quantum computing problem. For example, one of the ways that we measure the difficulty of a cryptocurrency protocol is by the key length. It's simple to increase the key length, which exponentially increases the difficulty of deciphering the cryptography algorithm or cracking a particular message.

Not only that, but many of the best cryptographers in the world are working on cryptocurrency projects, developing quantum-resistant algorithms that will allow users to move their coins from the legacy addresses to new quantum-resistant addresses. While the concern about quantum computers is valid, it won't be a problem for a long time and it will be solved.

Consider the term of your investment. If you're holding for 100 years, you might need to worry about quantum computers, but there are more pressing concerns such as how to pick a cryptocurrency that will still exist at that time. Ultimately, it will likely be as simple as moving your crypto assets from one address to another at some point in the future to take advantage of the quantum-resistant features that emerge. This fear is not a reason to avoid the asset class and miss participating in the tremendous growth opportunity in the meantime.

Cryptocurrency consumes too much energy

Most people are aware of this issue because Elon Musk tweeted about it.[28, 29] Elon Musk is highly intelligent, one of the top engineers in the world, possibly of all time, but he expressed a view in a couple of tweets that cryptocurrency is too energy inefficient. These statements garnered a great deal of attention, but what people usually forget is that Musk moderated his position four days later, after the North American Bitcoin Miners demonstrated that much cryptocurrency is mined with alternative and renewable energy sources.[30]

Yes, cryptocurrency may be using a lot of energy, but as compared to what? What is the total usage of power by all the banks in the world? How much energy is used to manufacture the paper for bank notes, mint coinage, transport it between banks, for all financial workers to drive to work? Everything uses energy, so it is important to compare the total energy impact of the alternatives fairly.

One exciting idea is that cryptocurrency creates a direct financial incentive for miners to find cheap, frequently renewable energy. Thousands of people around the world are mining cryptocurrency, from small graphics processing units in basements or dorm rooms all the way up to multi-million-dollar cryptocurrency data centers. Mining companies build these data centers with specialized computers to crack difficult cryptography problems (as we discussed under "Quantum computers will break the blockchain"). When they crack the code, a block is added to the blockchain and the miner gets a financial reward.

All these people are financially incentivized to do two things: build computer hardware that solves problems more effectively and decrease the cost of electricity. Either approach increases the hash rate per kilowatt hour, but increasing the speed of the hardware is becoming challenging as chip designers are running into physical limitations for how many transistors they can fit on a chip. As a result, decreasing the cost of electricity is a better strategy.

Electricity is not free, although many firms have attempted to decrease their energy costs to nearly zero. This might be by constructing their own solar arrays (a system of multiple solar panels generating electricity), partnering with petroleum fracking oil-well operators to capture natural gas that would ordinarily be flared into the atmosphere or purchasing underutilized power plants. While all of these approaches can lower the incremental cost of power, they are not zero cost.

One of the hotbeds for cryptocurrency mining is in eastern Washington State, where there's low-cost hydroelectric energy from a low-emissions source. This is perfect for cryptocurrency mining as it is uninterrupted (unlike solar arrays or wind farms) and low cost (unlike petroleum-based power plants). The only disadvantage is that hydroelectric energy is not available everywhere. It is limited to regions with substantial waterways.

Over time, the incentive to create more efficient wind and solar installations will put downward pressure on the price per kilowatt hour of renewable energy technologies. Cryptocurrencies create the perfect incentive to reduce the cost of electricity through renewable energy.

Increasingly, projects are moving away from the proof-of-work mechanism, by which Bitcoin operates, toward a proof-of-stake consensus method. In a proof-of-stake system, cryptocurrency network participants approve blocks based upon their relative ownership of the cryptocurrency tokens rather than by solving complicated energy-inefficient cryptographic puzzles. Ethereum, the number-two cryptocurrency project in the world, is migrating toward the proof-of-stake consensus model and others have deployed this approach successfully.

While energy consumption is a concern today, there are incentives within the industry to improve it over time. For investors who are concerned about this aspect of the cryptocurrency market, there are many opportunities to invest in projects that do not use the power-intensive proof-of-work method.

MINERS STOP NATURAL GAS WASTE AND CUT ENERGY COSTS

The natural gas left after an oil well has been fracked is considered "stranded" (too far from pipelines to be worth connecting) and is usually "flared" (burned) or "vented" (released into the atmosphere). Both processes are environmentally problematic, but Bitcoin miners in Texas have found a cleaner solution by using the stranded gas to power their rigs.[31]

One of the pioneers, Matt Lohstroh, is building mobile gas-powered rigs from a prototype created in 2016 by Canadian oil and gas engineer, Steve Barbour. One of Lohstroh's smaller "Giga Boxes" can hold $1.5 million worth of computing power, burning 87,000 cubic feet of gas a day, which produces enough electricity to power 720 homes. The larger boxes produce more than 450 times that amount. Around twenty smaller oil and gas companies have signed up for Giga Boxes and Lohstroh is enticing bigger companies by offering to buy their gas.

It's not backed by anything

This fear is based on an illusion that fiat currencies are backed by something. They're not; in the US, the currency was backed by gold, but that stopped in 1971. At this time, no world currencies are backed by gold.

People often ask, "What's the value of cryptocurrency?" because they think of it like a stock where investors can impute the value based upon the firm's earnings. Frequently, investors are willing to pay twenty+ times the value of the earnings for a stock, but Bitcoin and many other cryptocurrencies don't have earnings because they are not shares of an operating business. There are no dividends. Some tokens have dividends/rewards, but largely the change in price outweighs the value of the income.

A good example of investors still losing money even though a cryptocurrency paid a high dividend comes from the LUNA failure in May 2022.[32] Despite a 20–50% annual percentage rate, the value of the token fell to zero over six days and destroyed many investors' portfolios.

Think about cryptocurrencies as commodities that are priced by the market as opposed to valued. What's the value of a barrel of oil? Perhaps little if that oil is refined into gasoline and put into a teenager's automobile; perhaps a lot if it is used to power a factory that creates an income for the business owner and jobs for the community. All potential applications of that barrel of oil are reflected by the bids that investors place, which creates a market for the commodity that converges on a price based upon macroeconomic factors and speculative trading.

Oil and other commodities have a long track record, so the various valuation methods are well understood. For example, one of the common methodologies applied to gold, oil or other commodities is to measure the cost to produce it. We can apply a similar concept to cryptocurrency: what is the cost of producing one Bitcoin or one Ethereum? There is a production cost, as we discussed when we looked at proof of work and proof of stake, that can be calculated at any point in time. That is one perspective on the value of Bitcoin.

A second method is to look at the utility value of the commodity. What can someone do with 1,000 board feet of lumber? A 2,000 square-foot home typically includes around 12,000 board feet of lumber, so we can assign a portion of the value of a home to the lumber.

Similarly, if someone uses Bitcoin to send money, what is the utility value of that in aggregate? The SWIFT global payment network, which handles international wire payments between global banks, generates around $1.5billion in revenue per year. Perhaps cryptocurrencies could provide that function at a lower cost and some value could be imputed to this ability, which provides another perspective on the value of Bitcoin and other cryptocurrencies.

Then there is the speculative value. Because cryptocurrencies are not solely assets, but also technologies, investors often think about the value of the technology. For example, if we could go back to 1983 and purchase a block of IP addresses that other people would have to pay us to use in the future, that would have a certain amount of value. It's not obvious exactly how high the future value of a cryptocurrency asset is going to be, but the general direction of the world of technology suggests that it's going to be very high.

There is a tremendous range of views about the value of cryptocurrency. Some feel that it is valueless while others would place a nearly infinite value on the coins. This wide range of valuation perspectives contributes to the volatile characteristic of the asset class.

At this point in history, we can assume that the value of all cryptocurrencies will not be zero, but that tells us little about the value of an individual project's tokens. Investors swarm the markets, each with their own view, whether that is a cost of production, utility value or speculative value, and the cryptocurrency market price is the weighted average of their opinions at a precise moment.

Coins can be lost or stolen

Most cryptocurrencies are bearer assets. As you will know if you have seen the movie *Die Hard*, anyone who possesses a bearer bond can redeem it. Cryptocurrencies are like that, by and large, though instead of being printed on physical paper, they are stored digitally using cryptographic keys. If you lose the keys to your cryptocurrency wallet or they are stolen, that cryptocurrency is irretrievable. If you keep your wallet on your cell phone or home computer that others use, they can send the money to themselves or to an invalid address, which would make it equally lost, so this fear is legitimate.

Holders must take responsibility for securing their crypto coins and there are widely available technologies to achieve this. One of the first solutions to be developed was a hardware wallet. This is about the size of a USB flash drive and holds your private cryptocurrency keys so that they aren't on your computer. If you get a computer virus or someone gains access to it, they cannot access the keys because they're not on the computer itself.

Similarly, for investors who store their coins on exchanges, there is a risk that their password could be stolen. Most legitimate cryptocurrency exchanges use two-factor authentication (2FA) during the login process, which reduces the risk of an unauthorized user accessing the account and stealing the coins. The FIDO Alliance, which develops authentication solutions to reduce reliance on passwords, has promoted the idea of using a hardware token as an alternative to cell phone-based 2FA schemes so that individuals who have their phones stolen do not grant access to their cryptocurrency accounts to the thief.

Coins can be lost or stolen, but with the technologies available today, there is no reason for them to be. We will investigate the available solutions further in Chapter 8, "Operational Risks I: Technology".

Only criminals use it

There is a nugget of truth here. In its early days, cryptocurrency was indeed popular with drug dealers and cybercriminals on the dark web, but if we focus on this, we ignore the fact that cash can be used to commit crimes too. If we could compare how many crimes have been perpetrated for a $100 bill versus how many crimes have been committed for Bitcoin, it would be surprising if the US currency was not a far more common factor.

As the industry has matured, law enforcement and oversight groups have created programs to watch the blockchain for bad actors and flag certain addresses as tainted because they're known to come from a terrorist, money laundering or drug-related crime source. The criminal can't then sell those tainted Bitcoins on most exchanges due to the Know Your Customer and Anti-Money-Laundering provisions.[33] There is concerted effort to legitimize the industry and make it more robust, and the best firms are leading the charge on that path.

We cannot stop all crimes, but to focus on the few who are using crypto for nefarious purposes ignores the tremendous legitimate value provided by the technology.

It was invented by an anonymous person

No one knows who created the original Bitcoin protocol. There were only papers under a pseudonym of Satoshi Nakamoto with early online forum posts by this same shadowy character, so there is an air of mystery around the birth of Bitcoin. Some people find that spooky, but do you know who wrote TCP/IP, which is the protocol that the internet uses to transmit data? Do you know who built the HTTP protocol that serves webpages? Probably not.

The story is so tantalizing that nearly everyone has a theory. Conspiracy theorists think the protocol was created by the CIA or NSA, and some people think it was Hal Finney, an early Bitcoin adopter. Other people have claimed to be Satoshi Nakamoto, but nobody's been able to prove that identity, and it would be easy to prove by signing a transaction with some of Satoshi's Bitcoins, which remain unclaimed.

Ultimately, it doesn't matter, because the software itself is open source—everyone can look at the code. The best cryptographers in the world haven't been able to find any flaws in it. More importantly, the best criminals in the world have not been able to hack it. No one has ever stolen Bitcoin because the protocol or the network was defective; when Bitcoin has been stolen, it has been because someone's laptop was taken and the thief guessed their password, or because someone didn't secure their keys well enough. We have to separate the mystery surrounding the contribution of the theory by an anonymous person from the technology itself, which is robust and well audited.

Bitcoin was one of dozens of competing e-cash projects that were happening in the cypherpunk scene in the 1990s. Bitcoin may not even have been the best project that came out of that community of minds, but it became the most popular. While it is revolutionary in its application, all the cypherpunk projects were revolutionary; but it wasn't revolutionary from a technological perspective. Bitcoin uses standard asymmetric cryptography; a new form wasn't invented.

As a result, scientifically, cryptocurrency isn't new. It is taking well-worn ideas and combining them in an interesting way that makes a compelling product. In contrast, imagine taking an iPhone back to 15th-century England; everyone would say we were witches, but today, the cryptographic algorithms cryptocurrencies are using are well understood. We talked about the "magic internet money" level of understanding in the previous chapter, but there's no magic here. The captivating story about the shadowy inventor of Bitcoin ultimately has nothing to do with the technology that we're using today, although it would make a great TV series.

The government might ban it

The government can't ban a technology like this, although at the cryptocurrency exchange or fund manager gatekeeper level, it can make it difficult for people to redeem the coins. If the government were to close down Coinbase, which is one of the biggest exchanges in the world, that would affect the market price of Bitcoin tremendously because the liquidity would be far less and it would be harder to buy or sell.

Many totalitarian governments do try to ban Bitcoin. China has outlawed it in different ways over the years, banning mining and transactions in Bitcoin, but ultimately, it can't stop the proliferation of a technology. Imagine a government outlawing the screwdriver. It would never last because screwdrivers are useful. They could ban the sale of screwdrivers, but underground screwdriver rings would soon emerge, much as bootlegging operations emerged during the Prohibition era in the US. Much to the chagrin of governments, people will find a way to obtain something that is useful.

It would, of course, affect the market price if a large government, like the US, banned Bitcoin. That said, major US corporations like Tesla now own Bitcoin. If the price of Bitcoin is made to crash, the S&P 500 goes down. Also, US governments are highly incentivized to keep getting elected, which rarely happens for those that create economic destruction. Besides, cryptocurrency investors have created tremendous wealth and wealthy people have the means to influence public policy.

Governments also love tax revenue and cryptocurrency transactions are frequently the most heavily taxed in the world. Far from banning it, governments are more likely to treat cryptocurrency as a revenue source and we will see its integration into the traditional economy.

It's all rigged

If you believe this, the next two chapters on investing are for you.

People tend to lose money on stocks because they feel compelled to buy what is in the headlines. If you see any asset on the front page of the papers, making astronomical gains, that usually happens at the peak of a market. Undisciplined investors get excited and buy at the peak. All marketable assets have this problem, but it has more to do with human nature than the asset itself.

Consider the odds that the day you learn about a specific cryptocurrency, stock or investment is the best day to buy it. Everyone knows that markets go up and down over time and there are opportunities to buy at the lows and sell at the highs. The best times to make an investment are when no one's talking about the opportunity. That means educating yourself about cryptocurrencies and developing a long-term strategy.

Portfolio managers must think in terms of their asset allocation. Once you decide to buy cryptocurrency, the natural instinct is to buy it all immediately for fear of missing out on the opportunity. Don't do that. Divide your capital, be systematic in whatever you do and accumulate tokens slowly over time, or create your allocation with an algorithm that you think is suitable for you. It might feel painfully slow to do so, but if you're disciplined about it, you'll do well.

Summary

We have discussed the main fears you might have about cryptocurrency at this stage. Most are rooted in truth, but the industry is maturing enough to address them. In Part Two, we will examine how to mitigate more specific risks, but first, we will look in detail in the next two chapters at the decisions you need to make when you are ready to trade in cryptocurrency.

4

Products And Cryptocurrency Types

Let's imagine that you are ready to invest in a cryptocurrency portfolio. You've thought through some of the considerations outlined in the previous chapter, engaged the younger generation in the family and everyone is excited. You've decided to allocate 5% or 3%, or even just 1% of the portfolio to a cryptocurrency strategy. One of your first decisions needs to be: what product will you use to create that exposure?

Focus on your family's investing plan and what you hope your cryptocurrency allocation will contribute toward your goals. For example, a family hoping to achieve growth (the most common expectation) is likely to pursue holding individual cryptocurrencies over the long term. A family hoping to create income may opt to use DeFi protocols that open up opportunities for yield farming (more about that in the "Cryptocurrency types" section), or purchase proof-of-stake cryptocurrencies and stake them.

A cornucopia of funds and asset managers has emerged to create opportunities suitable for every family. The key to success is to make sure your cryptocurrency strategy truly represents your investment goals. The products available range from equities in cryptocurrency industry firms to venture capital (VC) to derivatives on the crypto market to the actual crypto tokens themselves. Focus on understanding the differences between them and how they can be combined to create the exposure you are seeking.

Understanding crypto equities

The primary advantage of creating an exposure to crypto equities is that investing (opening a position) is as simple as purchasing the ticker symbol—a unique symbol assigned to a security—through most traditional brokerage accounts. In addition, tax reporting is no more arduous than reporting your other investments.

There are a number of downsides, though. Creating a crypto exposure through equities is imprecise and leaves the position vulnerable to the business risk of the firm invested in, in addition to the cryptocurrency market. The firms' market price tends to correlate strongly with the market price of Bitcoin, but can suffer from multiple expansion during hot markets and multiple contraction during market crashes.

Ultimately, you do not own the cryptocurrency the allocation represents, so you do not have access to technological features such as staking, continuous markets (24/7/365) and direct transfer. Remember that by buying a cryptocurrency equity, you do not own the coins represented by the position and all assets of the firm may be subject to lawsuits or bankruptcy proceedings.

Crypto equities are especially suitable for families who would like to dip their toe in the water or have the business and technological acumen to dissect the financial statements and annual reports of firms and pick winners.

Equities at a glance

Advantages	Disadvantages
Simple investing	Exposure to business risks
Simple tax reporting	Unable to trade 24/7/365
Easy first step	You don't own the currency

GRAYSCALE BITCOIN TRUST (GBTC)

Grayscale is one of the oldest publicly traded cryptocurrency options, but the least generally understood. It is a private placement trust that trades like a stock over the counter. The trust purchases a certain number of cryptocurrencies and investors can purchase shares of the trust through their brokerage accounts.

This is an exciting proposition for investors seeking exposure to the tokens without the business risk of a firm, but the price of the trust shares is determined by the market. At times, GBTC will trade at a premium or a discount compared to the net asset value (NAV) of the tokens owned by the trust—sometimes, the premium or discount can be as much as 30%. This can be devastating for owners who wish to exit their position during a bear market, where the price of the cryptocurrencies the trust owns has already declined substantially. Then they can only sell their position for 70% of the NAV.

Understanding crypto futures

Futures trading combines high leverage with liquidity risk, so you must take a great deal of care when including futures in any strategy. This is doubly true when purchasing futures on a highly volatile asset class such as cryptocurrencies.

On the face of it, futures would seem to be an ideal instrument for investing in cryptocurrencies. They are highly liquid, they trade nearly twenty-four hours per day most days of the week, so are close to the always-on continuous primary cryptocurrency markets, and there is parity between the speculative asset class and the common speculative use of the futures contract. However, to understand the nuances of using futures to create your exposure to the cryptocurrency market, you need to look deeper.

One of the idiosyncrasies of the cryptocurrency futures market is that the contracts are not physically settled; rather, they are cash-settled. This means that the owner of the contract receives the cash value of the increase (or loses the cash value of the decrease) of the contract at delivery date.

This is not a way to purchase Bitcoin to be delivered later. It can be attractive to speculators who are primarily interested in the change in financial value of the contract, but investors who wish to create a long-term exposure will find themselves needing to "roll" the contract (sell a contract that expires soon and purchase one that expires later). This can add to the transaction costs of the position and since the contract is cash-settled, any technological features of the cryptocurrency asset are not available. In other words, there's no ability to transfer, make payments or receive income from staking or other DeFi opportunities.

Because futures contracts always have a settlement date, and the futures market has multiple settlements available for a given asset with multiple delivery dates, each contract settlement creates its own market with distinct pricing, volume and participants. Usually, the near-dated contracts set the prevailing price and the normal situation is for the near-dated contracts to have a lower price than far-dated contracts (known as contango).

That said, there are times when the far-dated contracts can decrease in value below the near-dated contracts (known as backwardation). The impacts of this change can be especially challenging for cryptocurrency futures as they are more prone to market swings, so in addition to the high volatility of the cryptocurrency market, investors must also manage the volatility of the individual futures market settlements.[34]

An additional challenge when you're seeking to achieve a cryptocurrency allocation with futures is that few cryptocurrencies are available in the futures market, so you might not see the specific project that you want to invest in for years, if ever.

A full-size Bitcoin futures contract costs approximately $250,000 in 2022:[35] a disadvantage for small accounts, but an advantage for family offices and high net-worth investors who need to deploy more capital. Bitcoin futures contracts can achieve this immediately, plus the contracts can frequently be purchased in traditional brokerage accounts, rather than you having to use a cryptocurrency exchange. Brokerages will often require additional approvals to make sure you understand the risks of Bitcoin futures contracts.

Managing a futures portfolio of cryptocurrency is much more complicated than just buying it and waiting. You could end up in a situation where you're buying the near-dated contracts frequently and having to roll them over every month or two months, depending on the release schedule.

Futures at a glance

Advantages	Disadvantages
Liquid market	Volatile market
Potential tax advantages	Trading 24/5
Uses existing brokerages	For long-term strategy, need to manage settlement dates
Simplifies tax reporting	Multiple transactions mean multiple fees

Understanding exchange-traded funds (ETFs)

An ETF is an investment company that is traded on a public stock exchange. This combines the simplicity of a mutual fund with the liquidity of a stock because the investors can buy or sell ETFs any time the market is open.

There are a number of cryptocurrency ETFs around the world, but as yet they are not available in the US. These funds often use futures contracts to achieve their exposure to the cryptocurrency market as opposed to owning the cryptocurrencies directly. This makes it easier to pass the requirements of the regulatory bodies because the futures contracts are better understood than the actual cryptocurrencies.

Because ETFs are essentially a blended instrument, they combine the benefits and disadvantages of both the equities and the futures products. They can be purchased directly in a brokerage account, which simplifies tax reporting, but they are constrained in terms of liquidity and ultimately the investor does not own the cryptocurrency, so the technical benefits are unavailable.

A key disadvantage of ETFs is that they cease trading at the same time as the equities market (4.30 p.m. EST on Friday to 9.30 a.m. Monday), so you aren't able to manage your risk for almost a third of the 24/7 cryptocurrency market trading hours. In a volatile market, it is frequently beneficial to be able to execute at any time to receive a fair price, and ETFs aren't there yet.

This is an example of how we in the crypto industry often feel constrained by the traditional financial markets because they're not operating 24/7. Our long-term vision is that all markets will trade 24/7 and the two industries will converge. That will be an advantage for family offices as increased liquidity will disproportionately benefit large accounts.

ETFs at a glance

Advantages	Disadvantages
Can be bought from brokers	Limited liquidity
Understood by regulators	Often backed by futures instead of tokens
Simple tax reporting	You don't own the currency
	Not yet available in US

Cryptocurrency exchanges

You can understand all these products in terms of the traditional markets, but how can you participate in a financial revolution by using traditional products? Experienced cryptocurrency investors consider holding the cryptocurrencies directly to be the gold standard. The best option, and the most common choice, is to buy on a cryptocurrency exchange.

Cryptocurrency exchanges vary in quality tremendously. The rule of thumb is the more complete the account verification process, the higher quality the exchange. Exchanges that do little to verify accounts are unlikely to have high-quality processes in other areas of their business, so will be more prone to unexpected problems. Some exchanges even accept anonymous cryptocurrency deposits and allow individuals to trade without verifying their identity.

For a family office, where transactions are often in six, seven and eight figures, you need a large, high-quality exchange with substantial liquidity. Otherwise, your orders will never be filled at a fair price. On smaller exchanges, just placing your order will move the market, and then the arbitrageurs will try to sell those tokens back to you at a premium.

Cryptocurrency exchanges aren't as well established as the traditional financial firms that most family offices and high net-worth individuals are accustomed to working with. There's a big difference between an unregulated startup company founded in 2011 versus a regulated banking firm founded in 1890.

In the cryptocurrency world, you must frequently balance your needs for exposure to the market with the risk of wiring funds to a startup company that may not exist next year. Whether you are buying directly on the exchange or working with an asset manager who is, you have to do your own research and due diligence to find an exchange that you trust.

When choosing a cryptocurrency exchange, first find out as much as you can about its internal operations, including SOC 2 compliance and insurance. Neither compliance nor insurance is a guarantee of a quality firm, but these are signs that it is operating in a professional manner, which reduces your risk.

Then, consider what tokens are available to you on the exchange's platform. Does it support the assets you need for your portfolio strategy? Thirdly, what is the volume for the markets you are seeking access to? Some cryptocurrency markets are more liquid on one exchange than another, so orders will fill better for specific tokens in different exchanges at different levels.

Owning cryptocurrencies yourself has technological benefits: you can divide them into hardware wallets or send them as payments. You can sign a transaction with your public address. If you are working with DeFi and executing one end of a smart contract, you will need to own the actual token. These technological capabilities aren't available to people who own shares of a derivative product such as a futures contract or an ETF.

A consideration is that cryptocurrency markets are dynamic and demand a certain amount of financial-trading sophistication. You need to know the difference between the various order types, understand how those are executed on your exchange, and be able to enter and exit your positions as cleanly as possible. This requires an in-depth knowledge of how cryptocurrency markets are structured.

Unlike traditional financial markets, which have consistent pricing across them, cryptocurrency markets are partitioned and only converge on pricing due to the profit-seeking behavior of arbitrageurs. In fact, the price between exchanges can vary by 1% or more due to erratic investor behavior.

Be aware that the exchanges can stop withdrawals at any time. If you own coins and keep them on the exchange, it's a great place to execute your trades, but you're at risk of having your account hacked or the exchange going out of business. Even for an SOC 2 exchange, which is insured, the bankruptcy process can take years—time in which your strategy can't be executed.

Additionally, there are frequently withdrawal or processing fees for taking your coins off of the exchange, as well as fees for executing trades, which can be quite high. Then there are blockchain fees, as well as transaction fees that are part of the blockchain network. If you want to trade daily or even weekly, it's likely you will leave your short-term trading holdings on the exchange. If you're focused on executing at a good price for a buy-and-hold investor, it makes sense to move your coins off of the exchange to take advantage of the good execution price while keeping custody of the coins and reducing your counterparty risk.

Finally, there's an obvious cybersecurity risk: if your wallet or your password gets stolen and someone accesses your account, they can transfer your cryptocurrencies off of that exchange. We will discuss how to mitigate this and other cybersecurity risks in Chapter 9.

Buying on exchanges at a glance

Advantages	Disadvantages
Buying direct is gold standard	Market requires complex knowledge
Continuous market 24/7/365	Huge range in exchange trustworthiness
Can move coins off exchange	Exchanges can halt withdrawals
Direct exposure to markets	Smaller exchanges can't meet family office needs
Exposure to more tokens	Exchanges can't protect against stolen wallets and passwords
Technological benefits of crypto	Fees to move coins on and off exchanges

Venture Capital investing

Many families are more familiar with VC investing than digital-asset investing, so they choose to obtain their allocation through early-stage investments in firms that they believe will benefit from the growth of the cryptocurrency market. These investments bear the normal benefits and risks of VC investing, chiefly an expectation that few of the investments will survive, but those that do will have such tremendous success, their rarity will be outweighed.

The challenge of crypto VC is that you are overlaying an already risky asset class with a strategy that has a high failure rate. Crypto firms are correlated with the market price of Bitcoin, so they tend to thrive in up markets, but fail during bear markets. It is rare to see the same firms during successive market cycles because VC funding dries up during the down markets and the firms cannot continue to operate at a loss without additional funding.

VC investments are by their nature highly illiquid. If you're investing through a VC fund, the typical lock-up period is five+ years, during which time the cryptocurrency markets may have been through one or two bear markets. If you're investing directly, liquidity may be unavailable for even longer. Five years in the cryptocurrency industry is a very long time indeed.

VC investing

Advantages	Disadvantages
Better understood	Illiquid
May have in-house capability	Stacks VC risk with crypto risk
One winner can offset losses	High fees for funds
	Low success rate
	Little protection from bear markets
	Need to understand both crypto and VC
	Deal flow is difficult to source

Cryptocurrency mining

Cryptocurrency mining is another example of investing in a private company, but bears mentioning because the opportunity is unique. Investors frequently pool capital to build a cryptocurrency mining facility and fill it with miners. The goal is to mine the tokens for less than the cost to purchase them and create a profit for the facility.

This works well in areas with low energy costs. The two chief inputs for crypto mining are energy and computer hardware, and there are only a few manufacturers of the hardware, so it quickly becomes a competition for the cheapest energy.

The challenges of cryptocurrency mining are many. The incremental income of each miner is often small, so the operation must be enormous, generally involving thousands of miners, to create significant profits from the mining activity itself. Most mining facilities will hold a certain amount of assets in hopes of appreciation, so they are tied to the market price of the assets they are mining. When mining facilities fail, it is because the investors have inadequately managed their capital reserves and have had to shut down during a downturn in the Bitcoin market.

Crypto mining investing

Advantages	Disadvantages
Simple business	Requires specialized knowledge
Potential tax benefits	Managing thousands of miners
Profitable during high markets	High exposure to crypto market price
Miners can be sold for a premium during bull markets	High failure rate during bear markets
	Mining technology becomes obsolete in a few years
	Taxation is complicated
	Dependent on energy prices

Cryptocurrency types

The original cryptocurrencies were a pretty straightforward token that could be exchanged across a blockchain network. They typically used proof of work as their consensus mechanism. The "magic internet money" level of understanding in Chapter 2 would be typical of this era where cryptocurrencies were primarily a transfer of value across the network.

The security of the blockchain network is still highly dependent on the hash rate of the miners applied to the network. This is because these miners control the hash rate, so get a say in how the network operates and can ultimately change the rules if they gain a majority of the hashing power.

In the early days, Bitcoin was the gold standard for a cryptocurrency of this type (a pure exchange of value) and Litecoin was developed as the silver standard, but Litecoin proved to be unnecessary because Bitcoin is nearly infinitely divisible. Throughout history, a gold and silver standard for coinage made sense because of a limitation on how much a physical coin can be divided, but this limitation does not exist for cryptocurrencies where the amount is divisible to eight decimal places.

Enter the smart contract

A smart contract is a cryptocurrency transaction with instructions or a set of rules attached. Once the transaction is added to the blockchain, those rules can't be changed, so the addition creates something completely new: a transaction that includes the rules, data and financial value all in one instrument.

In 2013–2014, Ethereum became one of the more popular cryptocurrencies that had a smart contract feature. Bitcoin had started to do this, but Ethereum advanced it with much more robust scripting and enabled the first wave of new cryptocurrencies other than Bitcoin, or altcoins. Ethereum is so flexible that a developer can write a contract and run it on the Ethereum network, but the contract creates its own cryptocurrency with a completely separate set of rules, ledger and ownership.

If you think of a Bitcoin transaction as a way to send and receive money as you would send and receive a message over email, Ethereum turned the blockchain into a computer which could make calculations. One person could send money to an address and the contract would fan that money out to other people or other smart contracts according to a predefined set of rules. This spawned a treasure trove of new applications for blockchain technology. New capabilities became possible and we had a cornucopia of altcoins, which led to the cryptocurrency wave of 2017.

As well as the original cryptocurrencies and the smart contract digital assets like Ethereum, we have new competitors such as Solana and Cardano. These projects have more utility and functionality than the Bitcoin style of transmittal cryptocurrencies and confer certain improvements over the Ethereum smart contract system.

DeFi

One of the new applications of these technologies is DeFi. DeFi projects are interesting as they often pay a yield for participating in the network in what's called yield farming. Think about this as income investing for cryptocurrencies. These projects can be like the dividend aristocrats of the equities market (companies that keep paying high dividends over years).

The attraction of DeFi is that you can create a theoretically risk-free or low-risk income stream. It could be a cryptocurrency token that's focused on a stablecoin type of project, pegged to the dollar or another strong currency or a basket of assets, and potentially paying a nice dividend (known as a reward). In practice, though, DeFi projects have a tendency to fail under stress, which can result in total loss for investors.

There's an amazing amount of innovation in the DeFi space. The idea is that at some point, all transactions—all financial instruments—will be converted to a DeFi token on a yet to be invented DeFi infrastructure, allowing us to do more complicated transactions than is possible in the traditional financial system or with the original wave of cryptocurrencies.

DeFi can make a lot of sense for cryptocurrency speculators who want to dig into the research and switch frequently between classic cryptocurrency tokens and DeFi tokens. While potentially lucrative, DeFi tokens can be less than ideal for systematic investors and their networks aren't yet big enough to absorb large amounts of capital, which can be another issue for family offices.

DeFi at a glance

Advantages	Disadvantages
Theoretically low risk	Can't absorb large amounts of capital
Innovative and exciting space	Increased risk of total loss
Useful for speculative investors	Less useful for core holdings
Potential for income from crypto	

NFTs

The principle behind NFTs, which emerged in 2020, is that if you can take a digital asset or real-world asset and attach it to a smart contract on a blockchain, you can prove with 100% certainty who owns it cryptographically. Smart contracts attached to digital media content, frequently images that are being sold on various online platforms, are being purchased by fans and investors who wish to own works by their favorite artist.

A key component still missing from these technologies is an effective royalty scheme that would allow the owner to collect a small royalty every time the image is used. One of the more compelling use-cases is token-gated communities: if you own one of the NFTs offered by the community manager, you have access to that community. This is presenting new and interesting ways for artists to commercialize their art, for communities to monetize their audience participation and even just as a filter for exclusivity.

The NFT space is promising and we have only seen the first wave of the applications of cryptographic proof of ownership. There are numerous real-world applications ranging from real estate title transfer to voting to collectibles.

What kinds of industries do NFTs enable? In years to come, we'll understand better how they incorporate into society as a whole, but for now, be aware that the market is very thin. If you buy an NFT, you may not find another buyer for it without taking a substantial loss.

One exciting application for NFTs is the idea of the metaverse, where digital assets are combined with virtual communities on the internet. An early example of this was the multimedia platform Second Life, which wasn't quite a video game, but looked like a game. You could go into a digital space and buy things with Lindens, the Second Life currency. Now we have sophisticated cryptocurrency and asset tracking mechanisms so we can create virtual communities where all of the objects in the environment are owned by someone and have novel financial behavior.

Is the metaverse going to look more like Zoom or Second Life? This is still to be determined. Right now, the metaverse appears to be the killer app for NFTs.

Whichever blockchain network ends up operating the metaverse will almost certainly benefit by being its backbone, but it's very speculative at this point as to which one it will be. Most likely, it'll be a token that hasn't been invented yet. No one can tell, so investing in NFTs requires a deep understanding of the evolving technology landscape around digital assets and the ability to hop from project to project quickly.

From the family office perspective, metaverse tokens and, to a certain extent, NFTs can't really absorb enough capital. If you want to invest $1,000 or $10,000 in NFTs, that's pretty easy, but to build an NFT portfolio that goes into millions of dollars is more difficult, because you have to buy a lot of tokens and the market is thin, which can result in tremendous losses.

NFTs at a glance

Advantages	Disadvantages
Promising space with many real world and metaverse applications	Thin market, so may be hard to sell
	Can't absorb much capital
	Royalty schemes immature
	Unclear what you own
	No legal rights

Gaming tokens

Avalanche (AVAX) is a platform where you can play smart contract games. One of the first games was CryptoKitties, written on the Ethereum blockchain. It was similar to a Pokémon-style card game: players would be issued a token that had certain properties based upon how much they paid for it, and they could compete with other players. Avalanche provided a similar mechanism on a fully decentralized app.

Now developers can create games where players win real value, for example by capturing an opponent's player. Think of the individual cards almost as pieces on a board: when players capture pieces, they can trade with other players or use them to play for themselves.

You can now play games directly on the blockchain, which is an area ripe for investment. Developers are launching games with wonderful artwork and talented teams, and there's a lot of innovation in the search for the killer app of blockchain gaming.

Gaming is more investable than the NFTs and metaverse tokens because real-world users are playing. The specific game pieces or any specific game may not be very liquid, but the platform that builds the game and the networks it builds the game upon are extremely investable.

As they're emerging, the networks are always going to be slightly beholden to the popularity of the individual games. As with NFTs, the best games may be built with a technology that currently doesn't exist.

Gaming tokens at a glance

Advantages	Disadvantages
Could be a metaverse opportunity	Depends on popularity of games
Attracts talent and innovation	Emergent, no clear winners
Growing space with rampant innovation	Gaming is competitive

Summary

Go back to Chapter 1. Start with an intentional vision of why you're investing in cryptocurrency, what you're hoping to gain and what risk-reward profile you want to achieve. An aggressive approach would be to focus on smart contract platforms that are having a lot of games built on them. A more conservative approach would be to only buy Bitcoin, or Bitcoin and Ethereum, the "blue chips" of the cryptocurrency world.

Depending on the exposure you seek to achieve, you must select appropriate products to create your exposure. Alongside this, you need to decide the best investment strategy that works with your product. We will investigate strategy in the next chapter.

Consider these factors when designing your cryptocurrency allocation:

1. Liquidity: can you enter and exit the market cleanly?

2. Growth: what is the potential for this specific cryptocurrency project?

3. Longevity: how long has the project been operating?

4. Importance: does the project have adequate community support and other investors?

Lindy's Law (named after the famous New York deli) maintains that the longer something's been in existence, the longer it's likely to be in existence.[36] For example, the idea of a restaurant where we sit with our friends and share a meal is rooted in an ancient tradition and we can almost guarantee that the experience will continue in some form for humanity. The half-life of tomorrow's new cryptocurrency may be quite a bit shorter than that. The average lifespan of most cryptocurrency projects is already fairly short, because most projects have failed or will fail.

Even if not fraudulent, cryptocurrency projects are often poor investments. In the 2017 altcoin boom, it was common for cryptocurrency projects to sell millions of dollars' worth of tokens without a functional product; just a promise and/or a white paper describing what the project was hoping to do. These projects predictably became valueless within a few years. In fact, most cryptocurrency projects that have ever existed are valueless, or could be perceived as valueless, or have retained only a small fraction of their peak value.

Of all the cryptocurrencies that exist and are popular today, only a handful of them—fewer than ten—were popular three or four years ago. It's common for cryptocurrency projects to follow a certain cycle. People get excited about them, they rise up the charts in terms of market capitalization and daily trading volume, and then they wither away over time. The smaller projects that are run by questionable teams are the hardest hit in a downturn.

As you learn more about the risks represented by new cryptocurrency projects, you will get better at choosing those that won't fail.

5
How To Invest: Strategies

We've considered how to invest in different products and cryptocurrency types. Alongside this, we need to think about investment strategies.

Think of an investment strategy as an asset plus the rules you will apply to gain exposure to the asset. It's important to consider it in this way because it is essential to have alignment between the investor, the asset class and the investment strategy. If any dimension lacks alignment, the investment will fail to fulfill its purpose.

This is especially true when you're investing in cryptocurrencies because the asset class is less understood. Many ideas we assume to be true in traditional finance can result in disaster for digital asset portfolios.

This figure shows the factors that need to be balanced to achieve the most appropriate portfolio alignment.

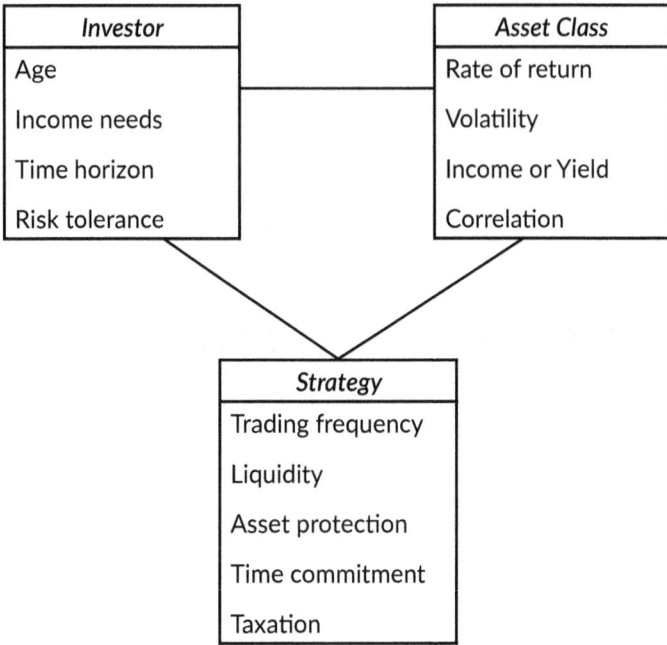

Investor		Asset Class
Age		Rate of return
Income needs		Volatility
Time horizon		Income or Yield
Risk tolerance		Correlation

Strategy
Trading frequency
Liquidity
Asset protection
Time commitment
Taxation

Investor, asset class and investment strategy alignment

Cryptocurrencies can be volatile contrasted with, for example, a federal or a government bond, which is insured by the government, so we need different investing strategies. Many investors purchase government or municipal bonds for their retirement portfolios to create a steady stream of income with low risk of loss of capital. A digital asset portfolio would be less suitable for this investor's needs because cryptocurrencies are highly volatile, although they can provide tremendous growth. Such a portfolio would be more appropriate for a younger investor who is focused on high-growth speculative assets or a family with a multi-generational timeframe.

We'll talk a lot more in this chapter about trading strategies, as opposed to buy-and-hold strategies or long-term holding strategies. To reiterate, that's because there's more to be gained by trading volatile assets rather than slow-growth assets.

For example, the S&P 500 typically has a 50% decline about once per decade, so the cost of managing it may not be worth it for S&P 500 investors. Cryptocurrencies, by contrast, have a 50% or higher decline nearly every year, so there is more to be gained by managing the declines.

Nonetheless, we will look at buy and hold first, as it's what most financial planners advise for beginning investors.

Buy and hold

Buy and hold is the simplest strategy as it doesn't require a great deal of knowledge. It is especially suitable for people early in their careers, or early in their wealth accumulation process, who need to protect the purchasing power of their savings while focusing on accumulating investable assets.

These investors frequently take advantage of the ETFs or index funds, which are diversified instruments so have some built-in risk management (the only risk management being applied). This works well for investors who are saving a small percentage of their income over many years to take advantage of dollar-cost averaging.

The investment needs of family offices and high net-worth individuals are different. Their income is frequently erratic; think of it as almost lumpy. Family offices tend to see an irregular series of large liquidity events, such as windfall profits or income from selling a business, as opposed to a steady income from a government job where the wages only change due to cost of living adjustments. The family office frequently needs to deploy a large amount of capital at once.

Buy and hold, while sound for many individuals, may not be suitable for family wealth. Liquidity events frequently occur during high markets, so times when the family is flush with cash may be the worst time to rebalance into other assets. Investing a sizable percentage of the portfolio in one lump sum would be a disadvantage.

One of the key advantages of buy and hold is that when the asset increases in value, there's no tax on the unrealized gain (at least in the US presently and in most countries). This is because there's a possibility that the value of the asset could also decrease in value. This creates a beneficial situation for families where they can grow wealth for many years, if they hold these assets, and the amount they would have paid in tax compounds along with the amount that they would have retained after tax, essentially earning a return on the government's money.

Typically, long-term holdings are taxed at a lower rate than short-term holdings. In the US, the short-term capital gain from stock trading or investment activity of less than one year is taxed as if it were ordinary income, while the long-term capital gains of assets that are held for more than one year are taxed at a preferential lower rate.

This is why, famously, Warren Buffett said his secretary pays a higher tax rate than he does.[37] Little of his wealth is being taxed because it comes from unrealized gains in assets that have not been sold yet, which is why he often says his favorite holding period is forever. That would mean that the investment is good and giving excellent returns and he's avoiding the drag that tax adds to the portfolio.

There is a downside to a buy-and-hold strategy for lump-sum types of distributions or large liquidity events. If you're deploying capital to a buy-and-hold strategy at the market top, you may not see the return of that value for many years. Investors who had a liquidity event around the market peak in 2000–2001 did not see their portfolio return to its former high in real terms (net of inflation) until 2021.[38]

This is a reminder that sticking with the buy-and-hold strategy through the fluctuations of the stock market takes conviction. When an investor purchases the index and the stock market crashes, they are totally exposed to that crash. People find it difficult to see losses in their brokerage account and psychologically it's tempting to sell during a period of market panic.

For example, in the 2001 financial crash (the dotcom bust), the Nasdaq 100 index, which many people owned as part of their stock portfolios, decreased in value by about 80%. Few people can see an 80% loss in their portfolio and not have an emotional reaction, which is usually most intense at the bottom of the market when the news media is the most sensational. These investors feel well justified in giving up on their strategy because they think the stock market's going to go to zero.

Having lived through both the Global Financial Crisis of 2008 and the dotcom bust, I understand the reluctance of people to put a lump-sum investment into a buy-and-hold strategy. It can be gut-wrenching to see the losses, but if that's their chosen strategy, investors must have the conviction to stick with it and act rationally when they see their life savings eroded by 50%–80%. Few people do, which is why so many investors lose money in those markets. Investment success is 80% psychological, 20% financial.

Success depends on your time horizon. Many investors felt cryptocurrencies were a bad investment at $20,000 in 2017 because they saw a 90% loss, but if they'd waited five years, they could have tripled their investment when cryptocurrencies peaked near $65,000 in 2022. Most investors would be happy about that return in any asset class, but because cryptocurrencies went down along the way, many sold at the bottom near $3,000 so failed to reap the rewards of their strategy.

Income strategy

Benjamin Graham, Warren Buffett's mentor, differentiated between a speculator (who purchases stocks in the hopes of capital appreciation) and an investor (who makes investments for the income or dividends they provide).[39] Income investing strategies are popular with older investors who look for stocks, bonds or real estate that will provide a steady income in their retirement. They can then reinvest to buy more shares, bonds or properties with that income, or they can use it to support their lifestyle. The idea is to create steady streams of income while preserving the original investment.

An income investor isn't looking for the price of the stock or asset to increase; they're looking for the income from the asset, above all else, and speculating that the dividends will continue to increase. There are a number of companies in the US that investors frequently buy into just for the dividend—companies like Procter & Gamble, where the dividends have been paid well over the years and continue to increase. These solid, mature companies that pay high dividends are commonly referred to as the dividend aristocrats.

This strategy is reliable in creating a source of income for the investors. The downside is that, if the company paying the dividend falls upon hard times, the dividends may be reduced or eliminated. The decrease in the price of the stock for the company may be greater than the total of the dividends the investor receives, so there is a risk of losing money.

Other investors use options contracts to create income. They can use a covered-call options contract to create income from a stock or a blend of owning an equity plus options contracts. In addition, there is an emerging opportunity in cryptocurrencies using the proof-of-stake consensus method, which pays a reward similar to a dividend to owners of that cryptocurrency operating a node (a computer running specialized software that helps the cryptocurrency network function) on the network. By having their proof of stake and supplying some computing power to the network, investors can receive more of that cryptocurrency over time.

Cryptocurrency staking is especially prone to short-term loss of value from the currency itself decreasing by more than the reward can offset over the short term. Cryptocurrency staking can also deliver outsized returns for periods of time, but investors must be cautious because the risk of total loss is higher than with more traditional financial assets.

Finally, there are numerous DeFi opportunities in the cryptocurrency space offering spectacular yields. Unfortunately, many investors mistake these high yields for free money as opposed to recognizing them as a risk premium in exchange for a risk of total loss.

Short-term trading strategies

To avoid unconstrained losses and the associated anxiety of the buy-and-hold strategy, and to find better parity between the asset, the investor and the rules for purchasing that investment (the algorithm), many people choose to use a specific trading strategy to create a different risk profile than is available with the long-term holding strategies. These sophisticated trading strategies require more knowledge and understanding than a buy-and-hold strategy, but may offer a better risk/reward profile, so they can be more appropriate for family-office clientele.

There are thousands of books describing different trading strategies, most claiming theirs is the best one, and financial YouTubers frequently make the same claim. This makes for brilliant marketing, but not sound financial investing. One of the downsides of using short-term trading strategies is that investors will hop from one to another. They try one for a limited period that coincides with a time when that trading strategy tends not to perform well, then they'll hop on to the next that produces similar results.

Even high-quality trading strategies have periods where they underperform, but repeating a strategy through good markets and bad creates a statistical advantage over a long period of time. Few investors have the discipline to learn multiple trading strategies and execute them through multiple market cycles, so they often rely on asset managers who operate hedge funds to apply the strategy on their behalf.

Trading strategies can be categorized in terms of different families. To select a strategy that is appropriate for the investor and the asset class, it is important to ask a couple of questions:

- Are the rules of the particular trading strategy consistent with the family of trading strategies?

- Is it giving a good representation of that trading strategy for that asset class for that investor?

Always consider all three levels:

- Is the algorithm right?

- Is the algorithm right for that asset?

- Is the algorithm right for that asset for that investor?

Even though most families will not create their own strategies, rather investing through funds managed by others, it's smart for family wealth managers to become more educated about the different types of strategies that are available. Then they're not creating overlapping allocations to the assets or the strategy. This is one of the reasons I advised in Chapter 1 that investors shouldn't be hostage to their deal flow. If they meet fund managers in their network who only follow one type of strategy on one asset class, they are not really diversified in their approach to investing.

Let's look at some of the main families of trading strategies.

Macro

A macro investor would look at the economic inputs and data—the price of oil and lumber and gold and various commodities—and try to predict, based upon that raw data, what the impact on the price of various assets would be. A macro strategy can be lucrative and there are many hedge funds, Bridgewater Associates being one of the most famous, that create an exposure to the market that results in a desirable risk/reward profile for families and institutions.

The macroeconomic factors of an economy tend to change relatively slowly as compared to the daily gyrations of the market. As the economy turns over a multi-year timeframe, macro strategies, when executed well, can participate in the emergence of new industries and large-scale changes in the economy.

A disadvantage of the macro strategy is that it really depends on the quality of the models, data and forecasts, and it can be prone to shocks from events that haven't been seen before. For example, the US in early 2022 had unprecedented low interest rates. A macro strategy that didn't take that into account may have been setting itself up for a tail-risk event (the chance of a loss caused by a rare event) that could have an outsized impact on risk.

Momentum/trend-following

These strategies focus on creating value out of the notion that markets tend to have momentum. If a market is going up over a period of time, it will continue to go up for a little bit longer. If the market's going down for a period of time, it might continue to go down for a little bit longer.

The momentum strategy has a number of advantages. It's somewhat stable across asset classes so works fairly well for many different types of assets. It can be executed in a number of different timeframes, whether you want to trade daily, weekly, hourly or monthly. Momentum investors sometimes apply virtually the same algorithm to a group of equities, commodities and currencies, and perform very well.

This strategy works for assets that are directional, i.e. they tend to have price movements that go in waves of upside punctuated by intense bursts of downside, like a large-cap technology or growth stock. A momentum strategy can create an exposure to that asset that captures a large proportion of the upside and a smaller proportion of the downside, which can be accretive to the balance sheet.

A disadvantage of a momentum strategy is that this cycle will frequently be less than one year, so the gains are often taxed as short-term gains. Also, a momentum strategy causes more trading than a buy-and-hold or macro strategy, incurring fees every time it enters and exits the market on behalf of the portfolio.

These strategies suffer during periods of sideways markets when the market is not directional, but range-bound (staying between a set of prices, maybe within a few percentage points of each other). The market is then prone to being whipsawed: perhaps the momentum strategy detects a breakout to the upside, but the breakout turns out to be false so it takes a small loss. Then it detects another breakout and the same occurs. This could happen for a period of time, creating a number of small losses that can be psychologically frustrating to the portfolio manager as they're seeing their capital drawn down while the market is basically neutral.

Momentum strategies are sometimes unreliable for instruments that don't exhibit trending behavior, but tend to have surprise price moves. An example would be the volatility index (VIX) on the stock market. The VIX is a calculation based upon how much volatility is happening for stocks if, for example, there's a news event that causes a great deal of consternation on Wall Street, where the prices of stocks will move up or down. That doesn't tend to trend well.

Another area where momentum strategies do not work well is when assets are prone to outsized moves based upon some news event or other external factor. Examples are long-tail alt coins in the cryptocurrency market (these are alt coins with low market capitalization and few network participants), or penny stocks in the equities markets (these are low-priced equities in the traditional stock market that have a reputation for being manipulated by traders).

Speculative assets such as cryptocurrencies are especially suitable for a momentum strategy, because the strategy would preserve a substantial exposure to the upside while limiting the downside risk and virtually eliminating the risk of being drawn down to zero. Basically, momentum strategies nearly eliminate the risk of total loss on the investment.

Mean reversion

A mean-reversion strategy is almost the opposite of a momentum strategy: it seeks to capitalize on the idea that what goes up must come down. If a price goes high above the prevailing price or what the trader perceives to be the intrinsic price, a mean-reversion strategy might short the stock (in the hopes that it returns to the mean, hence the name), and then capitalize on the price movement back towards the average.

These types of strategies tend to be short-term: more than a few days is somewhat unusual. They work really well in the sideways markets that the momentum strategies don't favor and can be very lucrative when the market is range-bound and bouncing from one local top to one local bottom over a period of time.

The disadvantage is that, as markets change from a range-bound time period to one that is more directional, the mean reversion strategies tend to struggle. As an asset is reaching the local top (and the mean-reversion strategy wants to short it) or local bottom (and it wants to go long on the asset), the strategy will see a series of losses if the market is directional to the downside or upside. Investors have to be careful about how much risk they're taking on a mean-reversion strategy and make sure that the risk is appropriate and they know their exit plan. Then, if the mean-reversion strategy creates losses, the losses aren't too large.

Mean-reversion strategies tend to be taxed fairly highly and create a lot of trading, which imposes costs in terms of time and fees. The assets that these strategies are suitable for are almost the converse of the momentum strategy: they work well with penny stocks or other instruments that tend to skyrocket in value over a short period, and then regress to the base price. This doesn't mean they can only be used for these instruments, but looking for markets that are trading sideways involves quite a bit of research. During periods where markets are directional (e.g. market crashes, recoveries or secular trends), there may be few opportunities for a mean-reversion strategy.

Statistical arbitrage

In pure arbitrage, a trader seeks to buy an undervalued asset that can be sold immediately for a profit. They want riskless opportunities to profit by buying and selling assets simultaneously in different markets. This strategy looks to capitalize on the difference between the price of two or more assets in different markets.

Statistical arbitrage is an extension of the strategy in which firms create complex statistical econometric models that seek to understand the relationship between different assets and notice when a mispricing occurs, then arbitrage the mispricing in the hopes that it will disappear. Then they keep the small profit. They can repeat this in many similar transactions, which is why statistical arbitrage is popular with high-frequency trading firms. It can have the shortest of the strategies' timeframes, frequently intraday, which makes this form of arbitrage a fairly low-risk one that can be repeated many times to create out-sized profits.

The primary downside is that it can be compli-cated. Most of it is done by computer algorithms; it is almost impossible to do manually. The more factors the econometric models consider, the more sophis-tication it requires to compute the relationships. In computer algorithm design, the least efficient algo-rithms are those that operate in exponential time efficiency, where each element is compared to each other element. This is commonly how correlations among multiple factors are computed, so these algo-rithms are often slow.

Like the other short-term strategies, statistical arbitrage has the negatives of taxes, fees and trading costs. In terms of hold time, it's the opposite of buy and hold: very short.

Summary

Now that we've discussed the various trading strategies, you can see how complementary they can be. If you blend a momentum strategy and a mean-reversion strategy, you could create a portfolio that makes money in most environments, whether the market is up, down or sideways. If you combine a macro strategy that capitalizes on long-term trends with a statistical-arbitrage strategy, you could potentially reduce your risk and increase your returns.

The family wealth manager's job is to find the optimal blend of strategies for their portfolio so that they can create parity among the trading strategy, the underlying asset and the needs of the portfolio or family. It's a complex task and part of it is understanding risks and how to mitigate them, which we will cover in depth in Part Two.

PART TWO
YOUR CRYPTOCURRENCY RISK PRIMER

Every family, every investor, every portfolio manager has to make decisions about how much to allocate to different asset classes, specific assets and strategies. To fulfill that role properly, you need a solid understanding of the risks involved in any specific investment. One of the challenges of being a cryptocurrency portfolio manager is that those risks are emerging, so they are not well understood.

In the traditional investment portfolios, such as equities, bonds or real estate, we've been learning the risks since the days of the Dutch East India Company. We have learned how to manage them and become well insured against them. The risk profile is now immensely knowable.

In the cryptocurrency world, we have a new asset class, with new threats and risks. As a bearer instrument, cryptocurrency presents a unique risk profile for investors that they may not be accustomed to. In this section, we will systematically examine the key families of risks and the mitigation strategies for each one.

Remember, not all risks can be eliminated in investing. Rather, it's the portfolio manager's job to understand and balance the risks to create a suitable allocation for the family they represent.

6
Market Risks

M arket risks are reflected by changes in the market price of the asset. They are the type of risk that is most understood by the public because they make headlines in the financial press. For example, when you hear a newsreader say, "The S&P 500 is down 2% today," they're talking about a decrease in the market price of the S&P 500 index.

In this chapter, we will examine some of the factors affecting market risk.

Risk: Price volatility

Price volatility is a measure of market risk where analysts assess the average daily change of the market price of an asset to calculate the standard deviation of that daily change in price. This daily standard deviation is widely regarded as market risk for traditional financial assets.

In traditional markets like bonds, the daily price changes are low, so they would have a low standard deviation and would be considered a low-risk investment. Equities and stocks would have a higher daily price standard deviation, so would be considered higher risk. By this measure, cryptocurrencies would be considered even higher risk—one of the highest risk assets available to investors today.

While financial advisors use the standard deviation of the daily price gyrations as equivalent to risk for their financial models, this is not the risk that investors feel. Most investors feel the risk of the maximum drawdown, from the peak of the assets valued in their portfolio to the trough when they hit the bottom.

Cryptocurrencies have a high level of risk from a standard deviation standpoint, but they're also the best performing assets of the past decade. This doesn't make sense intuitively because the standard deviation model for risk assumes that all changes in price are equal, but they are not. An investment that sporadically rises by large percentages is perceived to be just as risky as an investment that falls by large percentages, but an investor who's seeing a lot of upside standard deviation would be much happier than an investor who's seeing a lot of downside standard deviation.

It is more useful to characterize the risk of an investment strategy according to the maximum drawdown that the investment contributes to the overall portfolio, as opposed to the quantitative perspective of average standard deviation of the asset.

THE MAXIMUM DRAWDOWN VIEW OF RISK

When analyzing the contribution to portfolio risk of an investment, the portfolio manager needs three data points:

1. Average return
2. Maximum drawdown
3. Portfolio weight

Asset	Average return	Maximum drawdown	Portfolio weight	Expected return	Expected drawdown
S&P 500	10%	50%	70%	7%	35%
Gold	8.8%	42%	20%	1.8%	8.4%
Bitcoin	93%	80%	10%	9.3%	8%
Portfolio Total				18.1%	51.4%

When analyzing the portfolio's expected return and drawdown, we see that a small allocation to Bitcoin or other high-growth assets can create significant contribution to returns with similar expected drawdowns to the S&P 500. Despite the popular notion that digital assets have too much risk from a standard deviation perspective, the risk is more muted when viewed through a lens of portfolio drawdowns, which is what causes investors to panic.

TO MITIGATE

We have tools to mitigate the market risk of an investment, some of which we have already explored in Part One:

- Use diversification to reduce the business risk of a specific holding (the most common mitigating strategy).
- Use asset allocation to reduce the risk of portfolio exposure to a specific asset class.
- Use algorithmic trading strategies to reduce the risk of portfolio exposure to cryptocurrency or other high-growth speculative assets.

Risk: Too little liquidity/thin markets

Liquidity risk is the danger that an investor will not find a buyer or seller when they're attempting to enter or exit the market. It is one of the most underrated risks because most investors focus on price volatility, which makes sense when they manage small accounts in liquid markets where they are unlikely to be affected by liquidity risk. Family office and institutional investors must be more cognizant of the effect on their large accounts.

Liquidity risk is one of the more important risks that family offices and high net-worth individuals need to focus on, because they're deploying larger amounts of capital than the average investor. If they cannot enter or exit their positions cleanly, they stand to lose substantial pricing advantage in their investment portfolio. Many strategies that work with small accounts fail when attempted with sufficiently large accounts.

The cryptocurrency NFT market highlights this risk, as the market for a specific NFT may be robust or thin. In a thinly traded market, price discovery is less efficient and it's harder for investors to determine whether they're buying or selling at a good price.

THIN MARKETS IN REAL ESTATE

Thin markets are common in real estate. In a subdivision with many similar homes in a neighborhood on the market at the same time, we would consider that market to have a lot of liquidity. Buyers know what the prevailing price is because the market has ample examples of comparable properties. If they are buying a custom one-of-a-kind country home, buyers would be less assured that they're getting a fair price, because there are fewer comparable homes in the market.

The same is true for marketable assets, like equities, bonds and cryptocurrencies. The more robust the market is, the more reliable the pricing is for investors. For family offices investing large amounts of capital, it's valuable to consider the depth of the market as well as the price.

When Warren Buffett's company Berkshire Hathaway deploys a billion dollars, the market moves. It's difficult for it to enter and exit the market without the other investors noticing and trying to jump in front of it. While Berkshire is an extreme example, family offices are dealing with the same effect: when they trade in smaller assets, their millions of dollars often move the price of the asset. That's a liquidity risk.

The liquidity profile of assets differs a lot between asset classes. For example, cryptocurrency markets, which operate continuously around the clock and around the globe, have lower liquidity risk, assuming that the size of the investment was appropriate for the token being invested in, than the futures markets, which operate twenty-four hours five days a week. The equities markets (trading five days a week for eight hours a day) are even less liquid.

In real estate, the liquidity period is measured in months rather than days, as the buying and selling process takes a long time and a lot of due diligence has to be done.

TO MITIGATE

- Invest in high market capitalization assets that have high daily trading volume.
- Size your holdings against the market for the asset you are considering.
- Make sure your position is a small percentage of the daily trading volume.
- Use limit orders or over-the-counter brokers when entering or exiting a position to reduce price slippage on entry or exit.
- Construct portfolios so that the holdings provide sufficient liquidity for the needs of the family.

Risk: Market manipulation and insider trading

Market manipulation in cryptocurrency markets is not illegal; insider trading in cryptocurrencies is not illegal because they are not (yet) deemed securities. This is an area where the regulatory agencies around the world have fallen short and failed to protect investors.

Market manipulation is when a market actor performs an action that affects the price of the asset to their benefit. For example, a common market manipulation tactic is to use influence with the traditional or social media to generate stories that create anxiety for investors in the asset, so the actor can purchase it at a cheaper price. They later influence release stories that encourage a better price and thus benefit. This practice as it applies to traditional assets has been heavily scrutinized by the Securities and Exchange Commission (SEC) in the US for many years, but thus far, the SEC has failed to act on behalf of cryptocurrency investors.

Insider trading is where an investor (frequently someone within the company or related to someone within the company or a member of the US Congress) has information that is not public, but they trade on it for their own benefit. This is another area that has been highly scrutinized and regulated by the SEC for many years in the traditional financial markets, but not yet to protect cryptocurrency investors. There's no reason to expect these types of behaviors to stop, so investors must have a solid plan and be well equipped to deal with them.

SECURITIES LAWS

After the market crash of 1929, a number of laws were passed in the United States to raise ethical standards in the markets. The Securities Act of 1933 focused on the issuance of securities, mandating certain disclosures and making the firm issuing the security, as well as the individuals managing the firm, liable for a number of unethical behaviors.[40] The Securities Act of 1934 established reporting requirements and the SEC, and defined a number of forms of fraud.[41]

These acts have been effective at reducing fraud in the traditional financial markets because investors now have recourse against firms that employ unscrupulous business practices. That does not mean that there is no risk of fraud; only that if a firm behaves badly, the investor can pursue remedy in the legal system.

TO MITIGATE

- Develop a robust strategy that is unaffected over the long term by the whims of a celebrity on social media.
- Do not chase hot tips.
- Stick to your strategy through the many media hype cycles.
- Understand the product in which you are investing.
- Monitor the actions of the development team by subscribing to developer forums.

- Focus on assets that have a high market capitalization, because it takes more influence to move those prices.
- Avoid thinly traded markets.

Risk: Multiple markets, multiple prices

This is a specific risk that cryptocurrencies are vulnerable to. In the traditional equities market, there's a mechanism where new stock is offered in the primary market by an initial public offering (IPO) or, increasingly, through a direct listing. Once the primary market has been made and investors have purchased the IPO or the stock on a direct listing, then it can enter the secondary market where most trading activity occurs (where an investor goes to the New York Stock Exchange and buys a share of General Electric, or goes to the Nasdaq Stock Exchange and buys a share of Apple).

The cryptocurrency market works differently because it's highly decentralized. There is no central issuer, so there are two ways cryptocurrencies come into the market:

1. New cryptocurrencies are awarded to miners or stakers, so early investors—the developers of the protocol or the cryptocurrency network—own a disproportionate amount of the tokens.

2. A cryptocurrency development team does an initial coin offering (ICO), which works somewhat

similarly to the IPO, and uses the money from that to fund development and marketing of the cryptocurrency.

As the coins begin to enter the broader cryptocurrency market, there is still no one single market for cryptocurrencies. Each cryptocurrency exchange operates independently, so there is a market being made on each exchange on which cryptocurrencies are traded, and the price may differ wildly from one to another.

This creates the effect of not only slightly different pricing between exchanges, but different pricing in each country where cryptocurrencies are being offered. Exchanges in a country that has a more regulated perspective on cryptocurrencies may have a higher price than those in a country that is more permissive. Similarly, exchanges with poor reputations may have fewer participants willing to hold capital on their platforms, so the prices may be lower there.

Consensus develops around the price of the cryptocurrencies largely through the actions of arbitrageurs, who sell cryptocurrencies on one exchange and simultaneously buy on another exchange at a lower price, collecting a small profit. They collect this profit multiple times because they use advanced computer algorithms making many transactions per second, which helps the price converge across exchanges around the world.

Even so, price distortions still occur, especially during times of market volatility as investors become willing to sell their holdings at any price.

CASE STUDY: THE CARDANO PRICE DROP

On May 17 2021, the Cardano token ADA plunged by 55% intraday after an early investor placed a market order to sell a large number of it. This price action was mirrored throughout the other exchanges within minutes, which resulted in leveraged traders being liquidated, which exacerbated the crash. It took nearly ninety days for the price to reach a new all-time high as investors were understandably worried about the quality of that market.

Notably, the seller who triggered the crash did themselves a disservice by issuing a market order instead of a limit order or working with an OTC broker to facilitate the sale. A number of their assets were sold for a 50% discount due to their inexperience. Imagine selling your home and only receiving 50% of the prevailing value for it due to missing one element on an online form.

Summary

In this chapter, we have investigated the risks created by movement in the market price of the asset, studying price volatility, liquidity, thin markets, market manipulation/insider training and multiple prices in multiple markets. These risks all have parallels in traditional markets and most of them will be familiar to investors, but the difference is that because the cryptocurrency space is largely unregulated, there is little protection for investors.

As the markets move quickly, you are obliged to protect yourself through acquiring deep knowledge of them. You cannot rely on traditional or social media for this knowledge: the market intelligence that news stories focus on is usually out of date by the time you read it and could have an agenda that is not related to investors' best interests.

Remember that every risk can be mitigated to some extent. The decision for you as the investor is whether and to what extent to mitigate each risk, taking into account your investment strategy and how much you are investing while knowing that larger investments are more likely to affect the behavior of certain markets.

In the next chapter, we will examine risks created by the political and regulatory systems within which all businesses and investors must operate.

7
Regulatory And Governmental Risks

Any business or investment must operate within the confines of a political or regulatory system. Few families are extra-governmental (i.e. they have designed their offices so as not to be part of any nation state), so most are beholden to the whims of the current political system, the regulations that the government agencies impose upon them and the laws of the country in which they're operating.

This can sometimes create challenges, but frequently these limitations are better seen as opportunities. If a particular country provides an incentive for a certain type of investment activity, a global thinker would structure their entities to take advantage of that opportunity in that jurisdiction. Similarly, if a type of activity is penalized in a locality, a wise investor would avoid that type of activity in that locality.

An example of how government action can harm investors occurred in the US during the Great Depression.[42] Starting in 1913, the Federal Reserve had a mandate to maintain 40% of the currency value in gold reserves. During the banking panic and ensuing Banking Holiday of 1933, which was soon followed by a suspension of the gold standard, Congress rapidly repealed gold clauses in contracts and soon instituted a plan that purchased gold at fixed low prices from individuals who were no longer permitted to transact business in gold.

Once the government had reclaimed all the monetary gold in the US, it allowed market pricing of gold to resume and the price surged. People of means who had moved their gold holdings out of the US and offshore investors benefited from a tremendous price increase that typically US individuals could not access.

Governments can sometimes offer incentives through the tax code to benefit investors who are aware of it. An example is the basis step up on investments at death. If an investment is held for many years and increases in value, but is never sold, when the investor dies, the cost basis for that investment is set to be its value at the person's death. For the estate, this avoids a tremendous amount of capital gains tax on investments that are held for many years, encouraging long-term holdings of investments, which in turn encourages stability in the economy.

Any government uses carrots and sticks to encourage certain behaviors and discourage others. To be thoughtful investors, we must take into account the political, regulatory and legal environment in which we are making our investments.

Cryptocurrency is an emerging asset class with an emerging regulatory environment, so all the considerations outlined in this chapter are prone to change. The only thing that we can say for certain is that the regulatory climate is an area where families must continue to be vigilant to make sure that they are operating within the applicable guidelines and managing their investments effectively within that framework.

We will now investigate the most prominent risks related to regulatory and governmental conditions and discuss how and how far they can be mitigated.

Risk: Crypto outlawed

One of the big concerns that many investors have had, especially in the early days of cryptocurrencies, is that if a currency isn't sponsored by a government, can't the government outlaw it? This concern certainly has roots as there are already certain things you can't do with cryptocurrency. For example, you can't pay your taxes with it.

Could governments outlaw cryptocurrency? While technically it is possible, they'd be more successful banning the onramps and offramps to the industry as opposed to the technology itself. While fear of a ban on the technology may have been valid in 2012, it's less so now that the cryptocurrency industry has become a source of growth in the economy.

One of the challenges with understanding cryptocurrency is that it may be a currency, but simultaneously, it is a technology, which is radically more difficult to outlaw than a financial instrument. Governments can certainly make it more challenging to exchange cryptocurrencies for goods and services, but they wouldn't be able to eliminate it because people would just use it against their government's wishes. When there was an attempt to outlaw alcohol in the Prohibition era in the US, all it did was force alcohol underground and make it more expensive.

What could happen is price distortion in the market caused by large economic powers (like the US or China) stating that they are no longer going to permit cryptocurrency. Ultimately, they would have about as much luck as they would have with banning screwdrivers (to go back to our example in Chapter 3). Any attempt to ban technology that's so broadly useful and that many developers can replicate wouldn't be nearly as successful as governments may imagine, although they may well persist with the attempts.

The stablecoin type of cryptocurrencies, which are designed to retain their value over time, is a greater threat to governments' monopoly on printing currency. These cryptocurrencies provide an alternative and could be said to be inflationary because the government would no longer be the sole provider of currency. Hence the regulatory challenges that followed the attempt by Facebook to create a stable currency, called Libra (later Diem), that was backed by a basket of assets and currencies.[43]

This would have been a far more stable currency than the dollars and the pounds and the fiat currencies that central governments around the world are using, because it would legitimately be backed by assets instead of debts. It would also be more useful—24/7/365 transactions; instantaneous peer-to-peer payments—but government regulators applied pressure to the firms who had committed to participating in the network and the project was abandoned.[44] This is an example of how governments defend their monopoly on currency.

Another reason that it's difficult for governments to ban cryptocurrencies is because cryptocurrency projects have been in existence long enough to become popular. It would be political suicide to ban something that's so popular with constituents and in such wide use, especially as governments are frequently strapped for tax revenue. The more likely outcome is that governments may not welcome the cryptocurrency markets, but they will see them as a source of future tax revenue as opposed to something that must be quashed.

Technologically, they can't do it; politically, there are reasons why they shouldn't; and economically, most politicians are judged on the economic growth during their tenure. With major S&P 500 companies such as Tesla now holding cryptocurrency as part of their treasury, it's impossible for the US government to ban cryptocurrency without there being a drop in the stock market. Telling retirees that government action is going to reduce the value of their retirement plans and pensions and lower their quality of life is always going to be an unpopular move.

TO MITIGATE

- Hold cryptocurrencies in private wallets.
- Stay informed about the evolving cryptocurrency regulatory environment.
- Use algorithmic risk management to avoid a drop to zero if the worst happens.

Risk: High taxation

It is a real risk that governments could apply prohibitive tax on cryptocurrency transactions, because it's happening. Cryptocurrency transactions are treated as property in the US under tax law. Any purchases or sales, even exchanges from one cryptocurrency to another, are treated as a sale of property and subject to either short-term capital gains (which, in the US, is treated as ordinary income) or long-term capital gains (taxed at a preferential rate).

It would be preferable if the Internal Revenue Service (IRS) in the US would see cryptocurrencies as commodity futures contracts, with a 60-40 tax treatment under Section 1256 of the IRS code,[45] as well as allow investors to elect mark-to-market reporting (valuing assets by the most recent market price). As a trading asset, cryptocurrencies are not currently receiving any special treatment. They are being taxed about as prohibitively as any asset can be.

The top marginal rate in the US is about 39%. The 60-40 tax treatment decreases the rate to about 28%, which is still higher than the 21% long-term capital gains, but a big improvement over the existing trading tax systems. This especially matters for family offices because they're going to be trading in bigger blocks and hit the maximum marginal tax rate more frequently when they're buying and selling than an investor who is purchasing smaller amounts of cryptocurrencies.

Examples of the difference between the tax treatments of Section 1256 Futures Contracts versus crypto trading[46]

Gain	1256 Contract (60-40)	Short-term gains	Long-term gains
$1,000,000.00	$268,000.00	$334,072.25	$191,920.00

TO MITIGATE

- Operate in jurisdictions that treat cryptocurrency and cryptocurrency trading in a favorable light.
- Focus on high-quality cryptocurrencies that can be held for long periods of time.
- Use futures contracts which qualify for the 60-40 tax treatment.
- Hold cryptocurrencies in tax-friendly vehicles such as individual retirement accounts (IRAs) or private placement life insurance.

Risk: Infrastructure outlawed

Cryptocurrency tokens cannot operate without a robust network of participants running the project's software. Transactions are processed in a peer-to-peer fashion without any banking system or government involved, so there's a real threat that the government could take action against the infrastructure providers for cryptocurrencies. This has happened in China, where cryptocurrency mining has been outlawed multiple times.

Cryptocurrency mining is fluid, so if mining businesses are not permitted to operate in a particular locality, they will take their hardware and move. While this could cause interruptions, it's somewhat less likely to be a permanent problem than other threats to a digital asset.

In the US, public sentiment is currently against the cryptocurrency miners who help provide the infrastructure for the proof-of-work networks. Their high use of energy is perceived to lead to an increased use of fossil fuels, and therefore contribute to climate change. It's easy to foresee a politician believing that it's correct to ban cryptocurrency mining in their country to reduce pollution.

That said, a large percentage of cryptocurrency miners are using alternative energy, as we noted in Chapter 3, because electricity is one of their primary costs. There is, therefore, a financial incentive for miners to seek better-quality and faster alternative energy, such as solar, wind and hydroelectric power. In fact, cryptocurrency mining may even encourage the invention of alternative green energy sources.

TO MITIGATE

- Consider proof-of-stake tokens in your portfolio.
- Stay abreast of cryptocurrency mining regulations.
- Use algorithmic risk management to reduce risk of total loss.

Risk: No insurance

Because cryptocurrency isn't government-issued, it's not insured. In other words, it's not backed by the government's willingness to pay its bonds. Even the Securities Investor Protection Corporation (SIPC) insurance that is available for most brokerage accounts for stock and bond trading is not available for cryptocurrency exchanges. Therefore, any value held on exchanges or in a hardware wallet for the investor is not insured. There's no recourse if that value is lost; it will remain outside the traditional financial system.

This is less problematic for investors than it used to be because the quality of the exchanges and the financial institutions that are operating as custody partners has improved immensely. Nonetheless, it remains a risk that we have to manage (see Chapter 10 for more on counterparty risks).

TO MITIGATE

- Use credible exchanges with SOC 2 compliance.
- Partition assets among several exchanges and hardware wallets.
- Use insured third-party custodians.
- Manage your technology risks (see Chapter 8).
- Manage your cybersecurity risks (see Chapter 9).
- Manage your counterparty risks (see Chapter 10).

Risk: Government seizure

One of the features that make cryptocurrencies attractive to investors is that they operate outside of a corporate or governmental body. For example, a cryptocurrency doesn't require a bank's permission to transfer value from one individual to another.

Technology is not limited by government decree, so it would be difficult for the government to seize individuals' cryptocurrencies. However, the fact that many investors keep their crypto on a commercial exchange, either in their own account or through a crypto fund, makes it easier for governments to seize the cryptocurrency.

Government seizure or elimination of cryptocurrencies, with the exception of the stablecoins that are a direct competitor to government currencies, is currently perceived to be less likely than the other risks we've covered in this chapter. It is a lower-risk threat, but still possible.

TO MITIGATE

- Use a private hardware wallet and keep it secure.
- Operate in jurisdictions that are favorable to crypto.
- Use algorithmic risk management to manage downside in case the government announces seizure.
- Do not advertise your cryptocurrency holdings.

Risk: No one to sue

Because cryptocurrencies have a quasi-legal status in various countries, there is frequently little legal recourse when you're transacting business with them. You're often dealing with a counterparty that has no identification and exists an entire world away in an unknown legal environment. If you enter into a transaction with an unknown party, it's incredibly difficult to sue them for not performing.

This predicament is especially prevalent in the DeFi and smart contract world. If there is a bug in a smart contract that you're a party to, you have little legal recourse for suing the author of that smart contract, the network operators or the development team for that token. Many blockchain developers hide behind pseudonyms, which exacerbates the difficulty.

If you lose your keys (see Chapter 8), there is no one to sue. If you send a payment to the wrong address, there's no way to retrieve those funds. Thefts of cryptocurrency are not being aggressively investigated by financial crimes teams.

TO MITIGATE

- Understand what you are purchasing (cryptocurrency, DeFi, stablecoins, NFTs).
- Be skeptical of DeFi derivatives and leveraged instruments.
- Focus on well-established high-quality projects that have been vetted by millions of other cryptocurrency investors.
- Choose counterparties that have SOC 2 compliance or operate in reliable jurisdictions.
- Interact with digital asset firms in your home jurisdiction so you have basis for a civil suit.

Risk: Intellectual property claims

This is an area that a lot of people overlook because it hasn't yet come up frequently in the cryptocurrency world. There is a danger that any token that you've invested in may have a suit filed against it because it's impinging on someone else's intellectual property.

Because cryptocurrency projects are typically open source, the barrier to entry is low and many coins are derivatives of one another. For example, a copy of Bitcoin was made that eventually became Litecoin. If someone claimed intellectual property rights over the source code between the two coins (which they could, because the original source code was largely the same), that particular coin could be negatively affected.

Whether we ever see a lawsuit based on intellectual property in cryptocurrency remains to be seen, but given enough time and enough projects, someone will surely litigate. For this reason, it is wise to avoid coins that could potentially run into this type of problem.

CASE STUDY: GIVE A DOGE A (SIMILAR) NAME

While the software code bases for two coins will be different, the branding can be similar. In 2013, a coin called Dogecoin was invented with a logo featuring a dog—a Shiba Inu. Although it was designed as a fun side project, in 2021, it became worth billions of dollars. Inspired by the success and excitement in the Dogecoin community, someone else created a coin designed to capitalize on the same theme, called a Shiba Inu coin.[47]

Generally speaking, in intellectual property matters, the key questions are: are the two businesses in the same industry and could they be confused with one another? In this case, the answer to both of those questions is yes.

TO MITIGATE

- Focus on the top coins in terms of market capitalization and daily trading volume.
- Use algorithmic risk management to manage potential losses.
- Monitor the industry to be aware of potential intellectual property claims.

Risk: Future regulation

It's unknowable how cryptocurrencies will be regulated in the future. In the US, regulation could be controlled by the SEC, the Commodities Futures Trading Commission (CFTC) or a new body with an entirely new set of rules.

The risk, especially for family wealth, is that once your portfolio reaches a certain size, you could become a regulated entity. This will mean registering with either the SEC, like a hedge fund, or the CFTC or National Futures Association (NFA) as a commodity pool operator. If this occurs, the cost of regulatory compliance will be high. It's almost certainly going to require a high-quality audit, insurance, legal fees and enhanced reporting.

TO MITIGATE

- Partner with an attorney who specializes in cryptocurrency regulations.
- Professionalize the management of your cryptocurrency portfolio.
- Partner with a high-quality cryptocurrency fund that can manage these risks.

Summary

A certain amount of regulatory, governmental and political risks are unavoidable for all but a handful of family portfolios. While it is unlikely that governments will outlaw, seize or eliminate cryptocurrency, the climate can be made challenging for investors, exchanges and asset managers.

The most secure mitigation is governments' shared incentive to stay in power by not upsetting their electorate. The regulatory landscape as it applies to cryptocurrency is evolving, so an important element of mitigation is monitoring the industry and staying informed. Algorithmic risk management, focusing on well-established high-quality projects and SOC 2-compliant partners are other mitigation strategies.

The next three chapters focus on operational risk, specifically technology, cybersecurity and counterparty risks. These represent your mitigation against a significant regulatory risk: that most transactions come with no insurance and little or no legal recourse. There is usually no one to sue, so it's best not to need to sue anyone.

8
Operational Risks I: Technology

There are certain risks that we cannot avoid incurring when we operate any business or investment portfolio. In a more traditional type of investment, like private equity, there are recurring operational risks because an employee may steal money or a key supplier may be not able to deliver parts on time. In 2022, supply-chain issues emerged as an operational risk, disrupting the global economy.

As an emerging asset class, cryptocurrencies have a specific set of operational risks. They are frequently held directly by the owner, as opposed to being held in an account on the owner's behalf. Many cryptocurrency advocates believe that this is an advantage, but it takes a high level of technological sophistication to be able to manage these types of investments.

There are three main categories of operational risk as they pertain to cryptocurrencies. We will consider each one in this and the next two chapters:

1. **Technology risks.** Cryptocurrency is one of the first financial assets that operates solely on the internet. There is no physical hard copy of the Bitcoin network and even if there were, it would only be useful in conjunction with a network of participants. This implies a certain set of risks.

2. **Cybersecurity risks.** The network is operating largely on the public internet and involves a great deal of financial value. This attracts bad actors, from individual hackers to organized state-level attacks.

3. **Counterparty risks.** There is a counterparty risk whenever we have to trust a vendor or supplier or, in the case of cryptocurrencies, a custodian. As bearer assets, cryptocurrencies are especially prone to counterparty risks.

In this chapter, we will look specifically at technology risks.

Risk: Lost keys

This is the most common technology risk when you're operating a cryptocurrency portfolio. A feature of the cryptocurrency network that makes it safe for investors (no one can get access to your funds unless they have the key) also makes it dangerous (if you don't have your key, you yourself can't gain access to your funds). This places a higher level of responsibility on the investor than if they were transacting with a bank or brokerage account, which would be insured, or if their bank held responsibility for the custody of their assets.

All technology eventually fails, but if your wallet were to fail, all is not lost. Because the blockchain tracks which address owns what and the wallet only unlocks access to those addresses, wallets can be interchangeable if configured properly. Investors can and do create multiple wallets from the same private key as a backup in case one fails.

As a further backup, investors often write the keys for their wallets down and store them in a safe location. That opens up the risk of the keys being destroyed by fire, for example, so there are steel products designed to hold the keys even if the building burns down. Investors who own large amounts of cryptocurrency may partition their assets into multiple wallets so that even if one were destroyed, it would not be a total loss. By layering these techniques with an eye toward pragmatism, you can decrease your risk of total loss so you can participate in the exciting upside digital assets provide.

The goal of a risk manager is to identify opportunities to reduce the risk of financial loss to an acceptable level, although some risk always exists. Each step of your risk mitigation strategy needs to be focused on how much is at risk. An investor holding $50 of cryptocurrency would not purchase a $100 crypto wallet, instead accepting the risk of losing the $50 as if it were cash in their billfold. Family offices and high net-worth investors who hold hundreds of thousands or millions of dollars in cryptocurrency need more advanced strategies.

TO MITIGATE

- Educate yourself on how to protect your digital assets.
- Make sure you have good wallet backups.
- Protect your wallet backups as thoroughly as you protect your keys.
- Select a high-quality third-party custody provider with SOC 2 compliance and insurance.

Risk: Computer failure

If you hold cryptocurrencies on one device (in a wallet on your computer or your cell phone, for example) and that device is lost, damaged or stolen, the hard drive crashes, you forget to back it up or delete the wrong files, you will lose your cryptocurrency. The amount of the transactions family offices are making in cryptocurrencies is simply not appropriate for storing on a single computer that is not backed up or on a cell phone that could crash during a software upgrade, or be stolen or dropped onto the subway track.

If this happens to you, you won't be the first person. Billions of dollars' worth of cryptocurrencies are assumed lost because the early cryptocurrency miners or people who owned them had a hard drive crash or upgraded their computer and forgot to copy those files over. In fact, there are people who spend their days scouring landfills looking for hard drives, hoping that there might be cryptocurrencies on them that were thrown away and searching for the keys to unlock them.

TO MITIGATE

- Use a hardware wallet so the crypto is unaffected by computer failures.
- Create redundant hardware wallets so if one fails, you have a backup.
- Create backups of your cryptocurrency keys.
- Secure your cryptocurrency key backups in a safe location.
- Manage the physical security of your computing devices (see Chapter 9).
- Never use a public or shared device for managing your cryptocurrency assets.

Risk: Quantum computers cracking cryptography

We discussed this long-term risk in Chapter 3, but to recap, the idea is that in the future, computers will become so powerful that they will be able to decipher the secret keys for cryptocurrencies. There are a number of reasons that this fear is short-sighted, but primary among them is that cryptographers have already worked out a number of quantum-resistant encryption methods and expect to have quantum-proof cryptography in the near future.

The quantum threat is a good example of why investors coming from traditional finance have trouble managing assets in the cryptocurrency world. It takes financial *and* engineering acumen to be successful. Finance professionals don't see the technology threats coming, so they get blindsided by risks they weren't aware of. The primary danger for cryptocurrency investors is that the digital assets they have invested in are slow to adopt the new cryptography approaches or that the implementation is flawed (another technology risk).

TO MITIGATE

- Only invest in top-tier cryptocurrency projects.
- Make sure the development team working on the project is active and robust.
- Monitor the development forums for the projects in which you are investing.
- Engage with a competent asset manager who can do the above on your behalf.

Risk: Fat finger (sending tokens to a black hole)

This is a real and terrifying threat. It's an easy and common mistake, when you're making a cryptocurrency transaction, to mistype one digit in a twenty-seven to thirty-four-digit address. Was it...

34xp4vRoCGJym3xR7yCVPFHoCNxv4Twseo

Or was it...

34xp4vRoCGJmy3xR7yCVPFHoCNxv4Twseo?

If a Bitcoin holder enters the wrong address, even by one letter or number, they send the tokens to an address that no one has the key for. In other words, they are sending money to no one and it is unrecoverable forever.

This is a catch-22: the network was designed to be secure and anonymous, but without a central authority, we have to allow people to send money to any address and can't allow funds to be recovered. The side effect of this is that if coins are sent to an address no one has the keys for, there is no method for recovery.

There are numerous posts on forums every year from people who have sent cryptocurrencies to addresses that aren't in operation; or perhaps they are in operation and the recipient simply keeps the tokens. The odds are slim that if you mistakenly send a crypto transaction to an address that is not your own, that address will be used by another person, but even if that does occur, you won't know who the recipient is.

They might not even be in the same country as you, so you'll have no legal recourse.

Mistakes can happen in all kinds of transactions, whether you're paying someone else or transferring between your own wallets or a wallet on an exchange that you control and your personal hard wallet. Even when you're just reorganizing some coins and upgrading your security protocols or transferring money from your computer to your hard wallet.

TO MITIGATE

- Double, triple, quadruple check that the address you are sending funds to is correct.
- Perform a small test transaction on large transfers to verify the funds are received before sending larger amounts.
- Use copy and paste, but still verify the destination address. There are a number of computer viruses that look to hijack copy and paste.
- Use a hardware wallet that prompts you to verify the destination address.
- Calculate how much of your cryptocurrency portfolio you are willing to risk sending in a single transaction.
- Reduce the number of transactions that you make and make those transfers in a calm, focused and sober environment.

Risk: Limited utility

The price of cryptocurrencies is based upon their expected utility in the future, but that utility may currently be nearly zero. It can also decline over time, in which case many of the features of the cryptocurrency that you thought you were going to be able to use won't be available to you any longer. There are more dead crypto projects than there are active ones because so many fall by the wayside, and that means a lot of useless tokens or those with limited utility.

This is especially true of DeFi tokens and NFTs. These are secondary networks built on top of other cryptocurrencies and if there isn't adequate interest in them, then the DeFi token, for example, can cease providing the functionality it was intended to. Similarly, within NFTs, there is a prevalent idea that the tokens you own today will work with whatever technologies are going to emerge in the metaverse, but there's always the risk that they won't be compatible with the future platforms on which they need to operate.

TO MITIGATE

- Keep yourself informed about new tokens and platforms and make sure you understand the utility of the tokens you own.
- Focus on high-quality top-tier products.
- Monitor the competitive landscape of the cryptocurrency industry and shift positions as necessary.

- Use the cryptocurrencies you invest in to make sure they are making progress. If you don't have the technological capability to do so, engage a high-quality asset manager who has that knowledge and experience.

Risk: Network failure

In the traditional financial world, there's always someone willing to transfer your dollars for you and a bank that will accept them. There is always a way to move currency around the world. In equities, there's almost always a market for even thinly traded ones.

Cryptocurrency relies on a robust network. The miners and nodes that comprise a network collaboratively make it function so that the tokens or contracts can be transferred or executed. Because so many products have not passed the experimental stage, there are more cryptocurrencies that have non-functioning or weak (easily attackable) networks than there are robust and viable cryptocurrencies.

When participants stop using a digital asset, the network that processes transactions for it may cease to operate or operate so slowly that it becomes unusable. Imagine you had an automobile, but no roads to drive on or gas stations to refill the tank; it wouldn't be very useful. If you purchase cryptocurrencies that are becoming obsolete, you are at risk of finding the network fails in the long term.

TO MITIGATE

- Monitor the hash rate (in the case of proof-of-work protocols) and the staking pools (in the case of the proof-of-stake protocols).
- Purchase digital assets with high market capitalization and daily-trading volume.
- Monitor the engagement of the development team.
- Monitor the engagement of the users of the cryptocurrency.
- If you see any cryptocurrency that you own in decline, it might be time to remove it from your portfolio.

Risk: Rug-pull scams

This is similar to the old pump-and-dump scheme that has been pulled for decades in penny stocks, but in cryptocurrencies, the scammers do not have to accumulate the shares; they can create them from thin air, hype them, sell them and disappear. Rug pulling isn't illegal in the crypto markets yet, and there's no disincentive for scammers to ever stop doing it, so it's another area where dealing in cryptocurrency is like venturing into the Wild West. There isn't a lot of legislation, but there are a lot of people making a lot of money, so proceed with caution.

HOW RUG-PULL SCAMS WORK

People in chatrooms and forums on the dark web create a token that is essentially valueless, but they own a huge percentage of it. Then comes the hype phase. The promoters talk up the token or the asset and tell everyone it's going to be the next big thing, creating a sense of excitement almost to the point of fervor or fanaticism. We start to see an asset that we've never heard of before on television and YouTube.

Then comes the rug pull: new buyers come into the market and the price increases, usually astronomically because it's a low volume market and even a little bit of liquidity moves the price tremendously. As the new buyers come in, the rug-pull scammers sell their tokens off, and then there are no buyers left. The price crashes back down, usually to nearly zero, and the people who came in late lose a lot of money. Meanwhile, the people who orchestrated the scam make a lot of money.

This risk is especially prevalent in DeFi, where the cost to create a token is minimal and the promoters of the digital asset can hide behind pseudonyms and operate out of foreign jurisdictions where investors have little to no recourse.

TO MITIGATE

- Develop an overall crypto strategy that accounts for fraudulent projects and bear markets.
- Focus on high-quality tokens that have had their reputation for a long time.

- Don't be seduced by FOMO. Crypto investing can be lucrative, but not if you lose it all.
- If something increases in value suddenly, ask yourself why.
- Do thorough diligence on tokens and projects.
- Don't trust message boards or the financial media. Use primary sources of information.
- Be skeptical of all DeFi projects. Seasoned crypto investors see DeFi as an endless ocean of rug-pull schemes where an investable token is the exception, rather than the rule.
- If it seems too good to be true, it is. Whether you're investing directly or through an asset manager, don't blindly trust that the promises of the token will be fulfilled.

Risk: Forks

A fork is when the team that manages a crypto-currency product bifurcates and decides to have two versions of the software. For example, in 2017, Bitcoin forked into Bitcoin and Bitcoin Cash, which meant holders of Bitcoin had a Bitcoin Cash token as well.

In a hard fork, the project's blockchain is unified to a certain point, then a fork in the road occurs and the two blockchains operate independently. From that point on, there are two separate cryptocurrencies. This generates various risks. Primarily, if you have tokens that you are unaware of on both prongs

CRYPTOCURRENCY RISK MANAGEMENT

of the fork, it will be technologically complex to retrieve them.

The equities market has a similar feature when a large firm spins off one or more new firms (usually its divisions) from its existing business. The new firms trade independently regardless of their history and investors are typically granted shares of each of the spun-off companies, but the concept is somewhat unique in the cryptocurrency world because the assets themselves fork onto two networks. Investors who don't know the fork has occurred may have unclaimed assets residing out in the blockchain that they are unaware of.

As with all marketable assets, there is danger that the value of the tokens will become diluted because of the increased shares. Investors are sometimes deterred by forks because they don't know which of the multiple tokens are the right ones or which is the right leg of the fork to keep holding.

There's an additional risk here related to counterparties. If you aren't holding your own tokens and managing your own keys through direct custody, you may not even receive the extra tokens from the forks because some custody partners, exchanges or asset managers don't support the forked token. Also, each counterparty may choose one or other of the forks. If they choose the fork that becomes less valuable, you may find your financial value in that exchange reduced or eliminated.

TO MITIGATE

- Operate with top-tier SOC 2 compliant exchanges.
- Monitor the development news for your crypto holdings.
- Build the technological sophistication in-house or work with an asset manager who has the ability to claim assets from multiple blockchains.
- Save your cryptocurrency keys until you are satisfied that no value from forks has been missed.

Risk: Missed airdrops

Airdrops are somewhat similar to forks. They frequently happen when a new token is launched on an existing network, especially Ethereum or other smart-contract networks. The developers will "airdrop" tokens to increase interest (i.e. give everyone who owns Ethereum some of the new tokens, airdropping them into existing wallets). The risk is that if your Ethereum (for example) is being held on an exchange or through a fund manager, they won't give you credit for the airdropped tokens or your wallet might not support those tokens right away. Some airdrops later become successful projects, so you could lose out on a lot of value.

TO MITIGATE

- Stay informed about forthcoming airdrops related to tokens you own.

- Make sure you're using a high-quality custody partner and high-quality wallets that support many kinds of digital assets.
- Build the technological sophistication you need in-house or work with an asset manager who has the ability to claim assets from multiple blockchains.
- Save your cryptocurrency keys until you are satisfied that no value from airdrops has been missed.

Risk: No miners

Miners and staking nodes are the predominant ways of running the cryptocurrency network. If the miners find that it's no longer profitable to mine one cryptocurrency, then they may shift their hashing power to another project.

This commonly happens near the end of a project's life. The project may have had substantial interest for a while, but not panned out in the way that the investors and the people building businesses around the cryptocurrency were hoping. Over time, these projects wither on the vine and the network becomes more fragile and unusable because there isn't enough hash rate to add blocks to the blockchain. Additionally, this exposes the network to a potential 51% attack (see Chapter 9).

TO MITIGATE

- Monitor the hash rate or staking robustness of your holdings.

- Monitor the market capitalization and daily trading volume of your digital asset holdings.
- Select cryptocurrencies for your portfolio with robust development teams and network participants, and passionate communities.
- Be quick to shift to other digital assets if your holdings are not keeping pace with the market.

Risk: Smart-contract bugs

There are flaws in every piece of software ever written. Cryptocurrency smart contracts, which live on the internet, are no exception.

A cryptocurrency smart contract is immutable: that is, the contract can't be changed without tremendous effort and consensus from the owners of the token. That makes sense: you wouldn't want the terms of a financial contract to be easily malleable.

Just like a legal contract, a smart contract should be crafted with a great deal of attention and care, but they are being written by anonymous developers on the internet. These developers tend not to be working for large firms and may not even be working professionally in software at all; they may just be individuals writing contracts in a jurisdiction that you're not even aware of.

This is why flaws in cryptocurrency smart contracts are common. To combat the general low quality of smart contract software, an industry of auditors has arisen, but has done little to reduce losses by investors.

Many of the biggest DeFi losses have occurred with audited smart contracts.

This continues to result in investor losses. Because the contracts are public and anyone who is operating on that blockchain can see a copy, they're a juicy target for hackers, who are always looking for smart contracts with flaws that they can exploit. This most affects the more complex types of digital assets, such as altcoins, DeFi tokens, NFTs and digital autonomous organizations (DAOs).

TO MITIGATE

- Prefer audited digital assets over those that are not audited.
- Do not trust the audits absolutely; losses can still occur.
- Only invest in well-established assets with a robust user base and a long (relative to crypto) history.
- Monitor development of the smart contract platform for changes that could negatively impact your investment.
- Stay focused on your long-term cryptocurrency investment plan and don't get caught chasing "hot tips."

Summary

Although some risk is unavoidable, your goal as a family wealth manager is to identify opportunities to reduce the risk of financial loss to an acceptable level.

Each step of your risk mitigation strategy needs to be focused on how much is at risk. Where someone investing $50 may be able to absorb the loss of their investment, a family office manager dealing in hundreds of thousands or even millions of dollars will need a robust risk mitigation strategy.

In this chapter, we have looked at the operational risks around technology, along with some top tips on how to mitigate each one. Specifically, we have covered lost keys, network and computer failure, along with the perceived threat to cryptography from quantum computers. We have also examined the issues of no miners and limited utility, smart-contract bugs, rug-pull schemes, "fat fingers" tapping the wrong keys and sending your crypto into a black hole, forks and missed airdrops.

It's a lot to take in, but it's essential to be aware that these risks exist and mitigate the ones that are most likely to affect the portfolio you're responsible for. With that in mind, the next chapter will cover the much-discussed but always pertinent subject of cybersecurity.

9
Operational Risks II: Cybersecurity

Once people are aware that you have cryptocurrency, you become a target for theft and fraud. Cryptocurrencies are bearer assets, so whoever has access to them owns them. This makes them especially attractive to cybercriminals. As family offices are obvious targets, because they will frequently be deploying $1 million or more into their positions, you will need all the cybersecurity threat management strategies you would normally apply to your business, and then some.

In the cybersecurity industry, we often think in terms of attack surface: the more numerous and severe the vectors of potential attack, the more vulnerable we are to wrongdoing. Cryptocurrencies have a large attack surface for several reasons. They are typically open-source software projects, so there are opportunities for attackers to search the source code for vulnerabilities; the software is often written by anonymous developers and relies on an imperfect governance system; and these software projects operate on the public internet where they may be probed by anyone in the world. These risks are part of what makes our confidence in longstanding crypto projects like Bitcoin and Ethereum high: they have been in an adversarial environment for years, so whatever errors may have existed have likely been found.

Let's now take a look at the more common cybersecurity risks and some tips to mitigate each one.

Risk: Stolen keys and backups

As soon as you open an investment position in cryptocurrency, you need a strategy for securing your keys. This overlaps with your strategy for lost keys, which we covered in the previous chapter, but is worth examining separately.

Remember, if your keys are stolen, whoever has them can access your funds just as you can, and there's no restriction on what they can do with those assets. They can transfer them to another wallet that they own. They can use them for payments. They can send them to a black hole, just to be spiteful.

A major choice you have to make when designing any digital asset portfolio is whether to keep custody of the assets (and the keys) yourself, use a third-party custody service or use an asset manager for your cryptocurrency allocation. Using a third party opens up a number of other risks, which we'll talk about in the next chapter. As with most areas of risk, the steps you take to reduce one may increase another.

You must protect your keys even from people in your immediate social or professional circles. Because crypto transactions don't leave a paper trail, you would never be quite sure who had stolen your keys. If you're keeping them on your computer or cell phone and someone else has the password, they could make a copy of your keys and access your cryptocurrency assets from another device without your knowledge.

Another concern is a third party unknown to you hacking into your computer or installing malware that allows them to access your files, though this is far less of a concern than is widely perceived. It is much more likely that people close to you will steal from you or you will give your keys to a convincing fraudster.

MULTI-SIGNATURE WALLETS

Multi-signature wallets have helped to reduce the risk of attack. To execute a transaction, an individual needs a majority of the keys to sign the transaction before it can be posted to the blockchain. This is similar to a bank requiring multiple physical signatures on a corporate checking account (instead, you are requiring multiple cryptographic signatures).

This works well if all of your signing parties are using robust security protocols. An attacker would have to gain access to more than one key, with the backups for each key partitioned across multiple hard sites and, potentially, multiple geographic locations, before they can sign that transaction—a tough feat.

Multi-signature technology can be as simple or as complicated as you like. It could be two keys of three having to sign; it could be three of five or four of seven, depending on the amount of assets being protected and the sophistication of the organization managing them.

TO MITIGATE

- Match your mitigation strategies to the assets under management. Don't spend $100 on a hardware wallet to protect $10 worth of Bitcoin.
- Secure your computing devices with strong passwords that are only available to you.
- Use hardware wallets that hold keys separate from your day-to-day computing devices.
- Keep a backup of your keys and passwords in a secure location that only you can access.
- Partition your keys across multiple secure locations so only a portion of the key is available at each one.
- Use third-party custody solutions that have sophisticated practices (though this is also not without risks—see Chapter 10).
- Be discreet. Don't make yourself a target.

Risk: Exchange account hacked

This is a real danger that happens too frequently. If your account on an exchange website is attacked, it's similar to your bank account login information being compromised, except that there is no recourse. When someone sends Bitcoins or cryptocurrencies from your exchange account to another address, they're irretrievable. There is no bank to call to reverse the fraudulent transaction. There is no intermediary at all.

The higher-quality exchanges have SOC 2 compliance and insurance, but the insurance rarely covers mistakes on the part of customers. The only remedy lies in the legal system, but few lawyers understand digital assets and cases will take a long time to resolve.

There are two routes the attackers might take. The first is through the normal sign-in process on the website for the exchange, using a username and password; the second is through an application programming interface (API), which is how computer software programs talk to your exchange account.

In the traditional financial world, there are many computerized services that link to your bank account and download all the transactions for you. Similar firms have emerged in the cryptocurrency industry: they connect to your exchange account via an API, and can then perform usually limited types of transactions. People use them for monitoring account balances, for automated trading systems or to transmit accounting and tax information. All this is performed automatically by the software.

A critical problem is that API interfaces bypass 2FA systems, so they are especially attractive to attackers. Once attackers have accessed an exchange account through an API, they can make changes to your account programmatically without logging into the website. Depending on the permissions of the API key, the access may be wide-ranging; the attackers may be able to read the account balances and execute trades, or even submit withdrawals to their own account.

Even if the API keys only have trading permissions, they can still do a lot of damage, bleeding money out of your account into theirs. They usually do this by finding a cryptocurrency traded on the exchange that has a thin market (few market participants) and putting a sell limit order in their account for a hundred times the current value of the cryptocurrency. Then they'll enter a buy market order in your account that will purchase their coins at an inflated price, the net effect being that they sell their cryptocurrency to you at a very high price, while the prevailing price is maybe 1% or even 0.1% of the price you've paid. They execute the purchases in your account and sales from their account, so that leaves you with no value left. You still have the cryptocurrency, but you've overpaid for it tremendously.

This is often what is happening when we see a 10x–100x blip in a small altcoin. It isn't legitimate activity; it is someone being robbed.

Even an API key that only gives access to view account balances can be dangerous. If people know the size of the account, they know whether it's worth pursuing. This can lead to other types of attacks such as home invasion or kidnapping, which we discuss in Chapter 11.

TO MITIGATE

In general:

- Use 2FA.
- Use SOC 2 compliant and insured exchanges whenever possible.

When you're using third-party custody, maintain tight control of access to any exchange where you are keeping funds. Follow the steps below and you'll be a much harder target for attackers, so they will move on to someone easier.

For better username and password security:

- Use a non-descriptive username, not your name or that of your family office.
- Create a long, robust unique password that will not be guessed by anyone: twenty or thirty characters with numbers and symbols.
- Never reuse passwords on exchange accounts, even for multiple accounts on the same exchange.
- Never share passwords between websites, so you limit damage in case one service is hacked.
- Use 2FA so that even if an attacker obtains the password, they still can't get in.
- Do not use text messages for 2FA if more secure options are available. If you do that, your last line of defense against SIM jacking (when an attacker gains access to your SIM card) is an employee at the cell phone store or an offshore call center.

- Use authentication applications such as Google Authenticator so someone who is able to SIM jack your phone number cannot receive your 2FA codes.
- Use fast identity online (FIDO) keys[48] such as YubiKey for 2FA so that your second layer of authentication is not physically on your device.

For better API security:

- Use a different API key for every vendor partner or application that you're connecting to your exchange API.
- Monitor the media for news of hacked exchanges and be diligent in deleting API keys for those exchanges.
- Use highly sophisticated software vendors that have had time for their technology systems to mature.
- Do due diligence on any firm you do business with. Don't trust that the flashy website means that the internal operations are of equally high quality.
- Partition your assets across multiple exchanges or custody partners.
- Issue as few API keys as possible. There is no such thing as safe access by third parties to your account, even for the account balance, because you don't want that information leaking into the world.

Risk: Phishing/fraud

The good news is that your digital assets almost certainly won't be stolen from you by someone decrypting your password or hacking into your account, even with the most advanced hacking algorithms. The bad news is that you're far more susceptible to handing them over willingly when attackers use social engineering to con you out of your security details, and thus your coins, via an email or a phone call.

The classic example of a phishing attack is where an attacker sends an email that is designed to look exactly like those sent by a financial institution, telling you that you need to log in to your account urgently. You click a link in the email and are directed to a fake website that is cleverly disguised to look like the financial institution's site. As you enter your login information, the cybercriminal uses that information to steal funds from you. They are often able to replicate the 2FA, so even that will not save you.

Phishing attacks by email are common because emails are cheap to send. These social engineering attacks are not unique to cryptocurrencies, but they are especially dangerous in this industry. Even if your exchange is insured, the insurance won't cover the loss because it is due to your actions. That said, family offices are increasingly obtaining cybersecurity insurance policies that cover losses arising from their own flawed security protocols or mistakes.

IT CAN HAPPEN TO YOU

Before you believe it could never happen to you, consider that even the SANS Technology Institute fell prey to a phishing attack in 2020.[49] A single employee allowed the attacker to mirror their email account, exposing 28,000 records to the public internet. The attack was not discovered for months.

When even a premier cybersecurity education firm can be a victim of these attacks, have no illusions that your family office will fare better. Especially in a world of bring your own device (BYOD) where the device itself may be compromised by an attacker before it even enters the office.

Cryptocurrencies are a popular target for fraud, yet again because the transactions are immutable. If a target actively sends a cryptocurrency token to a fraudulent address, the only recourse available is through the legal system, which is slim when you're dealing in a 24/7/365 global market. When you are the victim of a crime you were complicit in, no insurer will pay your claim and no one's going to return your money. Your money's not Federal Deposit Insurance Corporation insured, either, because in the US, digital asset firms are not government-regulated depository institutions.

Like phishing attacks, fraud continues to be a problem on the internet, and especially when you're dealing with digital assets. A common example, usually on social media, is an attacker creating a fake account that looks like that of a well-known wealthy person, say Elon Musk. The profile will look convincing: the correct icon; a similar username (perhaps @elonmust); similar tweet histories, so you follow the account. Then you receive a message from the fake account that reads: "If you send me a Bitcoin, I'll send you 10." You send the assets to the scammer, but never receive the 10 Bitcoin in return.

Some well-known cryptocurrency personalities such as Vitalik Buterin, the founder of the Ethereum project, now pre-emptively state in their social media profiles that they don't give tokens away. Yet scammers steal millions and millions of dollars every year by pretending to be him or Elon Musk or whoever else is likely to gain them followers. It works, or they wouldn't do it.

There's very little you can do if you're the victim of a fraud. If someone tricks you into giving them your digital asset, it becomes theirs because it is a bearer asset. You can file a claim with the police, but the challenges remain: law enforcement doesn't understand cryptocurrencies; the attacker may not be in your legal jurisdiction; and tracing them may be nearly impossible. The best approach is to avoid being a victim of a fraud.

Remember that when an offer sounds too good to be true, it probably is. No one is giving away free cryptocurrency. The cryptocurrency market averages nearly triple-digit annual returns. If that isn't enough for you, then you need to moderate your expectations. Fraudsters make their living by taking advantage of others' greed. Don't allow greed to drag you into their trap.

TO MITIGATE

- Be vigilant. You will be bombarded by emails and phone calls from people who want to steal from you.
- Educate yourself on the types of attacks that are occurring. You can get up-to-date information from The Consumer Financial Protection Bureau (US)[50] and the Federal Trade Commission (US).[51]
- Never click on links in emails. Type the URL directly into your browser or, even better, use a bookmark.
- Use a high-quality email provider such as Google or Microsoft that has the resources to recognize and pre-emptively filter out many phishing emails.
- There are various email security tools you can purchase such as Avanan or Mimecast.
- Take a defensive posture on the internet. Assume that strangers have bad intent and no one is who they claim to be.

Risk: SIM jacking or swapping

A SIM jacking or swapping attacker duplicates your phone by getting the phone company to give them a new SIM card that's linked to your number. This is a pernicious attack because once the attacker has the SIM card, they can put it in any phone and receive 2FA codes sent over text message, which is a common security mechanism. They can also send messages as you from your phone number.

Many online services now use phone numbers as part of their password recovery mechanism and some are moving to a passwordless login. This means the SIM swapping or jacking attackers could reset the passwords for your email, and then log into it. Eventually, they could gain access to your cryptocurrency accounts on the exchanges.

TO MITIGATE

- Lock your phone number with your cell phone provider.
- Establish a PIN number on your SIM card.
- Always use 2FA if available.
- Use an authenticator application instead of a text message for 2FA. Only use a text message as a last choice.
- Use FIDO hardware security devices, such as the ones sold by Yubico.
- Register backup FIDO devices in case one fails.
- Secure your backup FIDO device in case of theft.

Risk: Blockchain doxxing

Doxxing means de-anonymizing someone on the internet, linking their real-life identity to their online identity. Before the public blockchain, only the bank (and maybe the regulators) knew who had how much money and in which account, but the blockchain is an open protocol. Most blockchain ledgers are public, but anonymous.

Increasingly, wallets and hardware devices are leaving an electronic trail as they're signing transactions. Plus, organizations like the FBI and the many world government agencies are writing sophisticated software to de-anonymize cryptocurrency transactions. The danger is that information that was intended to be private about your cryptocurrency holdings may become public.

This is especially dangerous for family offices and high net-worth individuals who are transacting in large volumes. There are websites focused on listing the top holders of cryptocurrencies (known as "whales") for people who are seeking to obtain an advantage by following their trading behaviors. Once your identity has been connected with a blockchain address, it becomes difficult and expensive to break that link because the blockchain is a graph tree where the entire history of every transaction is stored. If a wallet address becomes associated with your identity at any point, it is a simple task for software developers to create tools to associate future addresses with the original.

Beyond the normal privacy concerns, the danger is that the family becomes a target for crimes: fraud, phishing attacks or even kidnappings.

TO MITIGATE

- Consider the privacy features of the blockchain when creating your crypto allocation.
- Use a third-party custodian, exchange or asset manager so the digital assets will be associated with their firm instead of your individual identity.

- Educate yourself and your family, especially your children, on the human risks identified in Chapter 11.
- Partition assets among custody partners, exchanges and asset managers.
- Partition assets into multiple addresses if using self-custody.
- Be cautious about moving money between addresses that could be linked to your identity.
- *Never* post your crypto address or holdings on the internet. Create a new address for any public-facing payments.
- Never make payments from your primary wallet because the recipient will be able to see your balance.

Risk: 51% network attacks

This is where a group of people (or a government) seeks to gain control of a cryptocurrency project by purchasing a majority amount of computing or staking power. The cryptocurrency system keeps everyone honest by saying that no one can change the rules, but if a group gains control of 51% of the network computing power or hash rate, they *can* change the rules and do things that aren't supposed to happen on the network.

For example, they can explicitly deny transactions from certain addresses that they don't like or roll back transactions. Both of these would negatively affect the price for investors.

The larger networks are less prone to this type of attack because it's cost prohibitive: no one can carry out a 51% attack on Bitcoin because collectively, the Bitcoin miners are the largest computer in the world. What attackers can do is focus on a smaller project that has a $10 million or less market cap, which means the number of individuals, companies or governments that could take it over increases.

TO MITIGATE

- Monitor the hash rate (proof of work) or staking diversity (proof of stake) for your holdings to make sure that the network is healthy and has robust and diverse participants.
- Pay attention to small differences in the geography—how the network is being distributed across the globe—to avoid a concentrated exposure to political risk.
- Employ a trading strategy rather than a buy-and-hold strategy, so you can exit your position quickly.

Risk: Exchange denial-of-service (DOS) attacks

This is where a group of attackers renders a service unavailable by submitting a flood of requests to it. The attackers overwhelm the network architecture in such a way that legitimate customers can't transact business.

This sometimes occurs naturally when too many users wish to use a specific exchange. During the 2017 Bitcoin bull market, it was common for Coinbase to become unavailable for several hours at a time due to an overload of clients refreshing the screen. The fact that the largest exchange went down reasonably easily scared investors and caused panic selling (as you can imagine would occur if Bank of America's website became unavailable).

It takes little for exchanges to fall prey to this kind of attack during periods of peak volume. If you are pursuing trading strategies and you want to be able to exit your position when the market is going down and enter when the market is going up, a DOS attack inhibits your liquidity.

These problems are addressable, but the exchanges need sophisticated network teams to do so. As the digital assets industry matures, the firms operating in the space will continue to become more reliable.

TO MITIGATE

- Use high-quality, well-regarded, highly liquid exchanges that process billions of dollars' worth of transactions a day. They tend not to have problems like this.
- Use SOC 2-compliant exchanges. Although SOC 2 does not test network architecture capabilities, it does test the general maturity of the firm.
- Partition your holdings across multiple exchanges, just like you might keep money in multiple bank

accounts in case one bank fails and you can't get access to that money for a period of time.

Risk: Viruses and malware

Cryptocurrencies are prime targets for theft by computer virus because they exist entirely digitally. While I think it's untrue to say that Bitcoin is *only* used for crimes, it is attractive to cybercriminals because there's no banking institution involved that would require a physical presence.

If you are keeping your cryptocurrencies on your computer hard drive or cell phone, it's easy for a hacker to use a computer virus to steal those assets. The virus gains access to the hard drive, looks for specific types of files and sends them back to the hacker group. In this way, the hackers can access your keys. Even if you have your keys stored off the computer or phone (as suggested above), the hackers can change the addresses as you're copying and pasting them to re-route the transaction to themselves or a black hole, so they can do a lot of damage without your keys.

Most computer viruses and malware are installed inadvertently by the person who owns the device. They install software that is untrustworthy (browser extensions are notorious for this), or download a file from a phishing email or a piece of malware disguised as a useful application (weather applications are common culprits).

Even the cryptocurrency software applications could be vectors for malware and viruses. When you download the software from the cryptocurrency project to your hard drive and run it, you are trusting that its development team is competent and honest, but that is not a safe assumption with anonymously signed software from global development team members who know each other only by pseudonym. When you're transacting in multiple or experimental coins, there's a huge incentive on the part of software authors to distribute a package that has malware in it to steal your other crypto holdings.

CASE STUDY: ATTACKS THROUGH PROGRAMMING LANGUAGES

Every piece of software includes other software; very little is written entirely from scratch. People have to be cautious about not only the software they install, but also the software that's included in that.

An example of this was the attack on the Node. js system.[52] Node.js is an open-source computer programming language that uses a lot of third-party packages to gain more functionality. It has a package manager who downloads software from all over the internet, and then incorporates it into applications, so it often isn't clear what software is part of the Node.js project and what is created by third parties.

Event-stream was one of those third-party projects that was being downloaded 2 million times per week, but was not actively managed by the original developer. When an anonymous developer volunteered to take over the event-stream project for the original developer, it seemed a harmless offer until the new developer changed the software to look for Bitcoin wallets on every one of those 2 million downloads per week. The breach went undiscovered for two months (or 16 million downloads) until another developer noticed the change and reported it.

It wasn't even the main Node.js software that was perpetrating the theft; it was one anonymous person who added a few lines of code to this software. As soon as the project was updated, people's cryptocurrency started disappearing off their hard drives. Worryingly, there are still many legacy projects using this version of event-stream today.

TO MITIGATE

- Install antivirus protection on all computing devices.
- Make sure software updates on phones and computers are applied regularly.
- Be extremely cautious about the software you're installing on your computer.
- Don't click on links in emails, no matter how credible they look.
- Don't keep your crypto keys on your computer or phone.
- Only keep a small amount of cryptocurrency on your computer or phone—spending money.
- Have a computer that you only use for cryptocurrency transactions.
- Consider an air-gapped computer, which holds the keys, but isn't actually on the internet. Keeping the

core holdings entirely off the internet is a strategy
that most sophisticated exchanges use.

• Use virtual machines for experimental projects so
they cannot interact with one another.

Risk: Ransomware

Ransomware is a kind of malware through which,
instead of stealing or deleting the victim's files,
the attacker digitally kidnaps them and encrypts
them so the victim can't access them or threatens
the target with blackmail if the files are incriminat-
ing. Usually, the cybercriminal will leave a plain
text file that contains instructions for how to pay
the ransom, after which they promise to reveal the
encryption key.

Historically, this type of attack has been focused
on corporate files or database hacks that exposed per-
sonally identifiable information (PII) that would be
embarrassing for the corporation to admit had been
stolen, so now many companies purchase cybersecurity insurance policies against these threats.
However, this attack is especially effective with cryptocurrencies because they are entirely digital global
bearer assets.

Once the attacker locks the victim's cryptocurrency wallet, the money or coins in it are irretrievable
without a good-quality offline backup (see Chapter 8).
To further complicate matters, the ransomware attack
can come from any country, so tracking down the
attacker is challenging (see Chapter 7).

TO MITIGATE

The usual solutions that you know by now:

- Use a hardware wallet so that your cryptocurrency keys are not on your computer.
- Use a trustworthy SOC 2-compliant third-party exchange, custodian or asset manager (see Chapter 10).
- Revisit your backup policy. Make sure you have good-quality secure backups in locations only you can access.
- Partition your keys, with the separate parts stored in different secure locations that only you can access.

Summary

Among the challenges of managing digital assets is that they have both the financial risks associated with a marketable asset and the cybersecurity risks of a technology project. Ultimately, your cryptocurrency wallets are just files on your hard drive, unless you're using third-party custody, a hardware wallet or an asset manager. If you keep cryptocurrencies on your hard drives or mobile devices as a file, it's just a matter of time before they're stolen, because it happens to everyone at some point or another. A virus, ransomware, malware, phishing attack is going to happen to you.

You have to consider all these factors when you're planning your cryptocurrency storage procedures.

10
Operational Risks III: Counterparty Risks

The counterparties that cryptocurrency investors are most likely to deal with are exchanges. Exchanges, at least in the US and in most other countries, are unregulated. They aren't banks; they aren't insurance companies; they aren't government entities. They are private companies for the most part.

If you have an issue with an exchange, your recourse is similar to that you would have with any other private company, which is typically leaving bad reviews or filing lawsuits. There's spectacularly little legal recourse for victims of crimes perpetrated by exchanges or third-party custody providers. The duty falls to the investor to make sure they are working with exchanges of the highest quality and stay abreast of the news about the exchanges where they're holding large amounts of assets.

A good starting place is to look for SOC 2 compliant exchanges that are insured. Well-insured exchanges with a high degree of operational maturity are unlikely to lose control of their clients' funds, and if they were to do so, the insurance policy would eventually cover some if not all of the losses.

Some exchanges are now doing a much better job of operating with similar standards to financial institutions—pursuing SOC 2 compliance; becoming insured by third-party insurers; and developing quality financial controls—but you cannot assume that they will have the internal financial controls or hiring procedures that you would expect from a bank or regulated brokerage. There is no equivalent to a bank inspector for cryptocurrency exchanges and the barrier to starting an exchange is startlingly low. These exchanges are not financial institutions; they are startup technology businesses.

Ultimately, the only way to guarantee your coins will be secure is to take responsibility for holding your cryptocurrencies in your own wallet, preferably a hardware wallet with all the protections we discussed in Chapters 8 and 9. That's a complicated choice that requires a great deal of technological sophistication: disaster recovery, business continuity plans and cybersecurity procedures.

To employ a viable trading strategy, you need to trust in one or more digital asset exchanges, because the period while the position is open, the holding period, is typically short, so the risks and fees inherent in repeatedly transferring coins from crypto wallet to exchange and back again may be as high or higher than the risk of holding tokens on a high-quality insured exchange. Whether you're holding digital assets directly or through a crypto fund, you may well find that you need to work with an exchange. Ultimately, though, it doesn't have to be all or nothing. You can use an exchange for a portion of your cryptocurrency portfolio, an asset manager for another portion and manage a portion directly.

Let's examine the risks associated with cryptocurrency exchanges in more detail to help you ensure you are making appropriate trade-offs so you are less likely to be blindsided.

Risk: Exchange failure

Exchanges are businesses and businesses fail all the time. They go bankrupt. They become insolvent. They can be mismanaged. They can be put out of business by surprisingly high tax bills or government regulations. In addition, because cryptocurrency exchanges are businesses, they're not backed by the government as a bank would be. They're not insurance companies with actuarial reserves or government entities that can issue more bonds to support their balance sheet.

In a world where it's widely believed that 90% of all businesses fail,[53] by using an exchange, we're effectively investing money on a platform that is likely to disappear. We want to improve on those odds.

CASE STUDY: MT. GOX EXCHANGE FAILURE[54]

The most famous exchange failure was in 2014 when Mt. Gox suspended withdrawals and was eventually declared bankrupt by the Japanese government. Mt. Gox started out as a website where people could trade Magic: The Gathering cards, a popular collectible card game among technology enthusiasts. Then users of Mt. Gox began trading Bitcoin on the platform and soon the exchange was used entirely for Bitcoin trading.

What happened next is shrouded by rumors and speculation. What is clear is that at some point, the clients of Mt. Gox collectively had far more Bitcoins in their accounts than Mt. Gox had in its wallets. It is estimated that the exchange lost more than 25,000 of clients' Bitcoin. Accusations ran rampant that it was due to internal theft or an external hack. Everyone involved had a theory.

What risks caused so many Bitcoin to go missing?

- The exchange was operating with low-quality financial controls (counterparty risk).
- Many of the missing Bitcoin are believed to have been sent to black-hole addresses (technology risk).
- Mt. Gox operated in Japan where many US investors had little legal recourse (regulatory risk).
- Many investors failed to recognize the risk premium and transferred funds onto the exchange after withdrawals ceased in the hopes of purchasing Bitcoin at a discount (human risk).

Even in 2022 at the time of writing, the bankruptcy is unresolved. Clients of the platform are unlikely to be made whole, but there is an organized effort to distribute the remaining funds fairly to the holders.

When an exchange fails, the question becomes: what happens to the tokens held at the exchange on the customers' behalf? For many exchanges, the answer is that they don't know. Because the accounts are not held separately, each customer's account is basically a database entry that says how much they own, not unlike that in a traditional bank or other financial institution.

TO MITIGATE

- Use exchanges with a long track record.
- Use exchanges that are pursuing or have achieved SOC 2 compliance.
- Find out as much as possible about the exchange's insurance.
- Partition assets across exchanges, custody partners or asset managers so one counterparty failure does not result in total loss.
- Look for concentrated risks such as multiple asset managers using the same exchanges or third-party custody providers.

Risk: Internal thefts

This particular type of risk hasn't been thought about in finance for many years because the custody partners and brokerages have become such high quality.

In the emerging cryptocurrency industry, though, it still occurs. When you're using either a third-party custodian, cryptocurrency exchange or asset manager to hold your tokens, an employee may steal cryptocurrencies from the customer accounts.

Unfortunately, there's no way of avoiding this. A saying in the cryptocurrency world is "Not your keys, not your coins." If your tokens are being held on another party's wallet, you may own them by contract, but your custodian has possession of them.

By having possession of your tokens, exchanges can do things that sometimes aren't in your best interest. They may lend the tokens out to another person. They may use your cryptocurrency to cover shortfalls elsewhere in their ledger or they may simply steal them. Whether the owners of the exchange are complicit in this or not, there is always a risk that the management or the employees may act in bad faith and steal your cryptocurrencies.

This is an area that can't be managed perfectly. The best you can do is to work with high-quality exchanges that have good financial controls, make sure they're insured and get clarity on the insurance that covers them and for what types of events.

TO MITIGATE

- Use an SOC 2 compliant exchange with high-quality financial controls.
- Partition assets across exchanges, custodians and asset manager so that if theft occurs at one

exchange, it's less likely to affect your entire cryptocurrency portfolio.

- Use direct custody and manage your own wallet.
- Use multi-signature wallets. These are somewhat complicated, but they can help solve the internal theft problem.
- Use a decentralized exchange where all the exchange's liquidity is visible on the blockchain via a smart contract. This nearly eliminates the threat of internal thefts, but it often increases the threat of smart-contract bugs (see Chapter 8).

Risk: Front running

This is a dishonest business practice. It is technically illegal in the traditional stock market (although some would argue that high-frequency trading firms have commercialized it), but not in the cryptocurrency world.

It happens when an insider is able to see client orders before other market participants pre-empt those orders so that clients receive a worse price. For example, an employee of an exchange could see a large market order to buy Bitcoin, speculate that the size will move the market up, then enter their own order before the large one hits the order book and profit from the market reaction.

This is called front running because the insider jumps in line ahead of others in the order book. Digital asset markets are volatile and prices can move by up to 30% in a single day, so there's a high incentive for people to keep doing this.

TO MITIGATE

- Understand the nature of the cryptocurrency market. It isn't one market with one price, but dozens of distinct markets and prices.

- Use limit orders to set an acceptable price and limit the profits front runners can make at your expense.

- For family offices, whose order sizes will be large, consider working with over the counter (OTC) exchanges so your orders are not visible on the public order book.

- Size your orders appropriately so that they become a less attractive target for front runners.

- Accumulate large cryptocurrency positions over time, unless there is a specific trading strategy you wish to apply.

- Use highly liquid exchanges so your orders are a small percentage of the overall daily trading volume.

- Execute orders across multiple exchanges to reduce the overall size and limit the observability of them.

Risk: Withdrawal suspension

Imagine you make a large cryptocurrency investment on an exchange, you're trading and creating fees, and then the exchange suspends withdrawals. Theoretically, you still have an account balance with that exchange, but you have no way to liquidate it.

This happened with Mt. Gox (see case study earlier in the chapter). It happened in 2022 with Celsius Network,[55] and it will happen in the future with other exchanges that become insolvent. Rather than give everyone's money back, the exchange locks it up until it is able to wind up the accounts in bankruptcy court or find an acquisition partner who is willing to undertake its liabilities.

It's easy to foresee that if an exchange database was hacked, the exchange wouldn't know who owns what and would have to suspend withdrawals immediately. While you may theoretically own millions of dollars' worth of cryptocurrency, you wouldn't be able to retrieve it.

TO MITIGATE

- Use an SOC 2 compliant exchange with high-quality financial controls.
- Use multiple exchanges, custodians or asset managers so that if one suspends withdrawals, it doesn't result in a total loss.
- Use self-custody so the counterparty cannot cease withdrawals.
- Do not invest more than you can lose on any single platform.

Risk: Credit risk

In the context of cryptocurrency investing, credit risk is the risk that you won't receive what you paid for. Whenever you execute a transaction on a cryptocurrency exchange and buy ten Bitcoin, there's a small window of credit risk for the period of time between when you have contracted to purchase the Bitcoin and it's actually delivered to your account. You are giving the money to the seller and trusting that the tokens will be delivered.

This exists in the traditional financial markets too, where we commonly refer to the settlement process for stock brokerages as T+2, which is the trade date plus two days. This small delay is necessary so the brokerage, custodian, clearing houses and other parties can finalize the transaction. The process was developed over many years to ensure all the parties agree as to who owns what.

In the cryptocurrency world, settlement on the blockchain is a non-issue because the blockchain solves the problem, but when we're using an exchange, third-party custodian or asset manager, the transactions aren't settled directly to the blockchain. The exchange is performing settlement internally using its proprietary software. This increases the credit risk from a few minutes for blockchain settlement to whatever the exchange's internal rules are, and there is no guarantee that it will not change its rules in the future.

WHAT HAPPENS WHEN AN EXCHANGE GOES BANKRUPT?

We know a little about what happens when an exchange goes bankrupt from the Mt. Gox example (see case study), but that was a case where the funds had been stolen or lost. What if the firm is operating in good faith?

Coinbase, in its recent public SEC disclosures, noted that client funds could be seen by the bankruptcy court as an unsecured loan to the firm.[56] If true, this would be detrimental to customers with deposits on account at Coinbase. The financial press got it wrong and made it seem as if Coinbase suddenly had license to steal customer funds.

In actual fact, the only difference in this regard between Coinbase and every other exchange is that Coinbase disclosed the risk. It correctly recognized the regulatory risk (see Chapter 7) inherent in its business and notified its customers and investors, as is required of a public company.

TO MITIGATE

- Use high quality SOC 2 compliant exchanges that are more creditworthy.
- Know what the settlement time is for your exchanges and custody partners.
- Know what the redemption period is for your asset managers.
- Make sure that there is parity between your investing strategy and the settlement period for the exchanges and custody partners you're using for your transactions.
- Understand your asset manager's strategy for managing credit risk.

Risk: Loss of forks and airdrops

Forks and airdrops are features where the blockchain can periodically fork into two or airdrop tokens into accounts for existing wallet holders. The financial benefits of these events range from minor (in the case of airdrops distributed as part of a new cryptocurrency launch strategy) to substantial (as in the case of the Bitcoin/Bitcoin Cash fork).

When you're utilizing a third party through an exchange, custody service or asset manager, there is increased risk that they will not claim the airdropped tokens on your behalf or will choose the wrong branch of the blockchain fork. These choices are not in your control when you're using a third party, so you may lose money because of their incorrect choice (perhaps ideologically driven, as was the case with many Bitcoin Cash supporters, or more commonly due to limited resources).

The cryptocurrency industry is growing rapidly with new projects starting daily, so no exchange supports every asset. When you're entrusting a counterparty to hold your digital assets, understanding their history with forks and airdrops is an important factor to balance along with all the others in this chapter.

TO MITIGATE

- Use well-established counterparties that have a track record of claiming assets on behalf of their clients.

- Develop the technological capability to claim the forks and airdrops in-house.

- Monitor the upcoming forks and airdrops and consider self-custody during periods of time to claim those assets.

- Use permanent self-custody to be able to fully participate in forks and airdrops.

Risk: Lending

This is a fairly new type of risk that affects people who are trying to create income on their cryptocurrency portfolios. Exchanges or custody partners sometimes pay interest on cryptocurrency balances, just like banks do on cash balances in savings accounts, but as cryptocurrencies are a bearer asset, fractional reserve lending—the way that a bank performs it—isn't possible. Ultimately, cryptocurrency is moved to another wallet, to another account. By contract, it's supposed to be returned, but the obvious question is: how do you guarantee that it will be?

While you may have some certainty that it will be returned if the cryptocurrency exchange is operating in a high-integrity fashion, there's no guarantee. If you read the fine print in virtually all crypto lending platforms, it discloses this risk.

If a bank is lending on a home, it has a lot of security and the possibility of legal recourse. It can foreclose on the home or place a lien on it so it cannot be sold without the homebuyer clearing the debt. In cryptocurrency lending offerings, that isn't the case. There is little legal recourse. You can't foreclose on a cryptocurrency because it's a bearer asset that can be transferred around the world in a few minutes, so there's nowhere to go, nothing to foreclose upon. In other words, there's no capability to return that cryptocurrency to its rightful owner.

Margin calls are the other route by which you might lose your cryptocurrencies when you lend them out. Frequently, the cryptocurrencies are being lent to other customers who are trading on margin, which is a dangerous game. Cryptocurrencies are highly volatile and margin investing amplifies the volatility.

Margin is where you leverage your cryptocurrencies so that instead of being able to buy one Bitcoin, you might be able to buy five with 5x leverage, ten with 10x leverage. Some cryptocurrency exchanges even go up to 100x leverage, but if a client borrows 100x the cryptocurrencies that they have the cash in their account to support, their account would routinely be liquidated.

High margin traders often limit the amount of money on the cryptocurrency exchange, then take advantage of really high leverage to create giant returns for themselves. If the margin trader is successful, then their total risk is the amount of capital in their account, but the return is uncapped. People will do this to take a big shot on cryptocurrencies and see if they can make a lot of money, but if they cannot, their account will be liquidated and the lender will take the loss.

TO MITIGATE

- Do not lend your cryptocurrencies to others. If you do, recognize that the high annual percentage rate (APR) promised by the platform is a risk premium, not a risk-free return.
- Do not lend on platforms outside of your jurisdiction to ensure you have legal recourse if your funds are not returned.

Up until now, we have focused on counterparty risks connected to working with exchanges, but what happens when we decide to look beyond the exchange? What are the risks then? Let's have a look.

Risk: Fraudulent projects

Cryptocurrency tokens are usually the product of an unregulated open-source software project, managed by a group of anonymous individuals who are distributed globally. Add in low-cost promotion on social media and it's a perfect storm for fraud.

How do you know that the digital asset in your portfolio is being managed using the development team's best efforts? After all, these software teams are not fiduciaries, so they have no responsibility to act in their investors' best interests. Their governance structure is far less mature than we are accustomed to in the public markets and they're totally unregulated, so there is no reason to assume they are working for anyone's benefit but their own.

The incentive is incredibly high for developers to create fraudulent projects. Not only can it be immensely profitable, but many investors can't tell the difference between a great crypto project and one with slick marketing. As you don't know who these developers are or how to vet their projects, you have to be very careful about the types of cryptocurrency tokens you invest in. Even if the token is promising, remember that the developers might not operate in your best interests. They are making the rules and have the capability to change the software in ways that make the token less useful.

Developers frequently control a large majority of the tokens or hashing power, so a 51% attack becomes possible. Then there's the risk they will stop supporting the software so it ceases to work. They can create bugs that harm owners of the cryptocurrencies or include malware that steals your other cryptocurrencies when you install their software on your hard drive. When investing in a digital asset project, you are placing tremendous faith in the team that manages it.

TO MITIGATE

- Develop a formal diligence process for adding assets to your portfolio.
- Monitor the development forums for complaints by other holders of the asset.
- Stick to high market capitalization and high daily trading-volume projects.

- Make sure the development team members are as invested in their project as you are.
- Use top-tier exchanges that typically perform some level of diligence before adding tokens to their platforms.
- Ignore "hot tips," especially those coming from social media.
- Develop a comprehensive investment philosophy and stick to it even when the market is frothy.
- Engage an experienced asset manager who has the expertise to screen projects on your behalf.

Risk: International counterparties

Cryptocurrency, like all technological advancements, is an international phenomenon. Not only are specific cryptocurrency projects distributed around the globe, but so are the exchanges, the custodians, the asset managers and other parties you may be working with: wallet, technology and data providers.

All of these can create risks that are hard to resolve if the counterparty you're working with is not in your region. Contract law is regional, so the laws in your home country may not apply to the jurisdiction where your counterparty is. It is important to be cautious when conducting business internationally.

Because so much business is now conducted on the internet, it isn't always obvious when your counterparty is outside of your legal jurisdiction. To further complicate matters, many local counterparties outsource substantial portions of their operations to foreign employees to save money.

TO MITIGATE

- Insist on local counterparties for exchange, custody and asset-manager relationships.
- Prefer local counterparties for other support services.
- Clarify with your counterparties which portions of the service are performed locally versus being outsourced overseas.
- Understand the corporate structure of your counterparties to be sure they aren't using shell entities to protect them from legal consequences.
- Understand the legal jurisdiction in which counterparties are operating to be sure they have modern and compatible legal systems that provide adequate protections for foreign clients.
- Select high-quality counterparties who have a track record of reliability.

Risk: Stablecoin failure

Stablecoin failures are rare, but catastrophic when they occur. Stablecoins are cryptocurrency coins designed to be pegged to a specific currency or basket of currencies. It is important to distinguish between collateralized stablecoins versus algorithmic stablecoins.

Collateralized stablecoins operate much like classic depository institutions inasmuch as they receive

$1 and issue a $1 stablecoin. No currency is created or destroyed. The net change in money supply is zero, so the impact on markets is small.

Algorithmic stablecoins are much more like modern banking institutions where a small percentage of the coins are backed, but the majority are created and issued without backing. Usually, the stablecoins have a well-thought-out process for how they can maintain their peg to the US dollar, but they are less secure than collateralized stablecoins because they are not backed 1:1 by currency or other assets.

Algorithmic stablecoins become problematic when investors fail to differentiate between the stablecoin and the currency it is intended to represent. Many exchanges hold customers' balances in cryptocurrency stablecoins rather than in actual currency because it is technologically easier to work with. For example, exchanges that transact in US dollars directly have to manage liquidity over weekends and holidays when traditional financial markets are not available. With a stablecoin, they can offload the responsibility for liquidity management to the stablecoin project team.

The danger, of course, is that stablecoins are not actual currency issued by any government. Instead, they have similar characteristics to most other cryptocurrency projects: they are software projects with shaky governance models created by a global team of anonymous developers. Even if you're trading and sell all of your cryptocurrencies, but your exchange holds your balance in stablecoins, through the negligence, incompetence, criminal or fraudulent actions of the stablecoin project managers, you may well have some exposure to total loss.

CASE STUDY: AN UNLIKELY RISK?

The Terra project developed an algorithmic stablecoin that became popular during the bear market in 2022.[57] The project's team created two tokens: UST and LUNA. The thesis was that UST could always be converted into US $1 worth of LUNA, and so would always be worth $1.

The project became incredibly popular and investors flocked to it, believing they could stake the UST and earn 20%+ APR without incurring risk. Most investors believed this was a risk-free investment because they thought UST was equivalent to US Dollars. LUNA surged in value rapidly, becoming a top-ten cryptocurrency by market cap.

This worked well during the bull market in 2020 and the sideways market of 2021, but the bear market of 2022 revealed a fatal weakness. If the total market capitalization of LUNA dropped below the total number of UST that had been issued, it was possible for there to be a "run on the bank" where not all UST were backed by LUNA.

In May of 2022, the worst-case scenario occurred. UST holders began accepting less than $1 for their so-called stablecoins and panic ensued.[58] LUNA and UST both declined to effectively zero in fewer than six days, taking down Celsius Network, a popular crypto lending exchange; Three Arrows Capital, one of the most trusted crypto hedge funds; and Voyager, a Canadian publicly listed cryptocurrency firm. This triggered the notorious "Crypto Contagion" crash, where liabilities became so entwined that firms toppled like dominoes.

Worst of all, many families who'd believed they had found a loophole to get 20%+ APR on their money without risk saw their investments wiped out. These investors' greed and focus on market risk blinded them to the tail technology risks (Chapter 8) and counterparty risks (this chapter) of their investment.

This overemphasis on market risk is a common theme in scenarios where investors end up with a total loss, whether during the 2008 global financial crisis with credit default swaps or during the 2022 Crypto Contagion crash with stablecoin staking schemes.

TO MITIGATE

- Know how your exchange, custody partner or asset manager handles cash balances. Are they held in US dollars, a stablecoin or another currency?
- Understand the collateralization of the various stablecoins you may be exposed to.
- Recognize the difference between "risk-free return" for staking stablecoins and a risk premium that is offered because the stablecoin is less secure than government-issued currency.
- Protect your cash position as well as your speculative positions, so all of the usual exchange protections have to come into play: an SOC 2-compliant exchange with a long track record and high-quality management that redeems accounts in a timely fashion.

Risk: Trading and network fees

Trading fees are the cost of executing a transaction on an exchange or with an OTC broker. Every time someone buys or sells a cryptocurrency, there is a corresponding fee, just as stockbrokers used to charge a fee for every transaction.

These fees can change at any time. As an extreme example, if a crypto exchange increased its fees to 10% per transaction, that would be a 10% loss to your account when you try to sell cryptocurrencies on its platform. Then you're faced with a choice between withdrawing those tokens to redeem them elsewhere or taking the loss. Currently, this risk is small because cryptocurrency exchanges are in a competitive business and the prevailing direction for fees is down as opposed to up, but you still have to be aware of it.

This is one area where large accounts benefit. Typically, exchanges give fee discounts for large accounts, so a person who's executing millions of dollars' worth of transactions per month would receive a lower trading fee (in terms of percentage) than someone executing a few thousand dollars.

Network fees are specific to cryptocurrency networks and are part of the mechanism for how cryptocurrencies are moved around on the blockchain. They are paid to the infrastructure providers, usually miners or validators who process transactions and add them to the blockchain. During periods of peak activity, cryptocurrency networks, especially those with few participants, can slow down. To increase the likelihood of your transaction being processed, you may have to increase the fee you're willing to pay.

The danger is that as the risks we've discussed in this book or even new risks emerge, they could cascade. If a cryptocurrency exchange was hacked and a large number of customers chose to withdraw their funds, the fee required to do so may be much higher than normal. Again, this would tend to be less problematic for large accounts because, as a percentage of the transaction, the fees are lower.

During the emergence of Ethereum in 2017, so many teams were building on its smart-contract platform that the fee to execute a transaction on the network was around $40.[59] This made it unusable for smaller transactions; it was cheaper to move money with a bank at that time.

TO MITIGATE

- Monitor fees when trading and balance the other risks of using an exchange with the fee component.
- Keep up to date with what cryptocurrency trading fees are on your platforms of choice.
- Monitor network fees for assets in your portfolio, as they can vary widely between different projects.
- Select strategies that trade infrequently.
- Move assets between wallets as infrequently as possible.

Risk: Protocol changes

Cryptocurrency networks are essentially software projects that run on the internet across many computers. Just as you can't run a piece of software from years ago on a modern computer because the programming interfaces are different, changes to the networks may adversely affect your investment portfolio, up to and including total loss of funds.

There is a risk that at some point, a team that manages a cryptocurrency software project will make changes that are disadvantageous to the investors. Contrary to the example I gave above, where the Ethereum team worked to lower fees so that the network would become more usable, it's possible that a project maintainer may create higher fees to enrich themselves or otherwise change the rules of the network for their own benefit. Changes to the network may make it less desirable and affect the price of the cryptocurrency in ways that will result in losses to your account.

Even with large projects, you want to make sure that you understand the major protocol changes that could happen. For example, there's an emerging protocol on the Bitcoin network called the Lightning Network that allows for much faster, much cheaper transactions than at present (which is a benefit), but relies on lightning nodes (nodes that hold lots of cryptocurrency and have a contractual obligation with the other parties in the transaction). Those nodes will become a great vehicle for attack and the transactions will be less anonymous, so you may find that the risk profile is quite different to before Bitcoin had the Lightning Network.

The Kin token provides another example.[60] The project originally launched on the Ethereum smart-contract network, but in 2017, it chose to leave, which necessitated the conversion of the Kin tokens to the new network. Investors who were unaware of this and did not convert by the deadline risked losing their investment.

TO MITIGATE

- Make sure that you're working with high-quality cryptocurrency projects and monitor the development process to stay abreast of the latest changes to network protocols.
- Invest in large, well-known projects that have effective communication with their investment communities.
- Avoid small fringe digital assets where changes could be made quickly and without your knowledge.

Summary

In this chapter, we have covered the counterparty risks associated with exchanges and those beyond exchanges. Exchanges, at least in the US and in most other countries, are unregulated, so there's spectacularly little recourse for victims of crimes perpetrated by third-party custody providers. It's down to the investor to make sure they're choosing to work with exchanges or counterparties of the highest quality and stay abreast of the news about the exchanges where they're holding large amounts of assets.

In relation to exchanges, we have examined the risks of exchange failure, internal thefts, front running, withdrawal suspension, credit risk, loss of forks and airdrops, and lending. We then went on to look at risks associated with counterparties other than exchanges, including fraudulent projects, international counterparties, stablecoin failure, trading and network fees, and protocol changes. With all these risks front of mind, you must be wondering what to do about them. It is not hopeless; for every risk there is a mitigation tip, so you and your family can invest with confidence.

11
Human Risks

There are certain risks that you cannot manage in the same way you manage most risks in the cryptocurrency space. These are the risks that are unavoidable if you are human and live in the real world (the world outside the internet, which hackers cynically call "meat space"). We all have human frailties that can be exploited, and that automatically increases our exposure to risk.

There is a gap, for example, between theoretical cryptographic security and the actual level of security you can enjoy, because ultimately, you are the weak link. You can be subject to phishing attacks. You can have your passwords stolen. You can forget to back up your coins because you are tired.

You can shed some of the responsibility and employ someone to do the demanding skilled work of managing your family's assets. Later in this chapter, we will look at how best to do that, but of course, that asset manager will be human too. Make sure their processes protect them as well as you.

Let's now take a look at some of the more common human risks associated with investing in cryptocurrencies.

Risk: The psychological strain of the market

There is always a risk of making bad decisions because of the sheer psychological wear and tear of trading in a market, especially a market that can be tremendously exciting, but also tremendously depressing at other times. If you manage this psychological risk well, it increases your opportunities tremendously. It is perhaps the most important risk to learn to manage.

One way many investors respond to the market is to buy at the top, perhaps after seeing a lot of media coverage about cryptocurrencies or the latest hot asset. It's common for investors to pile on to it when the hot asset appears, but this almost always happens when it's already at the top. It's getting media coverage because it's at the top or scammers are nefariously seeking to create hype.

The sensible time to invest is when an asset is at the bottom. When the market is at its peak, it's too late, but it's human instinct to chase after the next big win.

This instinct is not limited to the cryptocurrency space; it has existed for many years in the traditional financial world. Even though everyone knows that gambling is almost certainly a losing strategy, people still gamble because a flaw in our psychology means random periodic rewards keep us humans engaged. We see patterns where they do not exist and think we can beat the system.

Slot machines use this trick to keep players playing long into the night. If a slot machine never pays out, players will realize they are losing their money fairly quickly and won't play for long, so game designers give players wins at random. Then the players will play for hours, chasing that next win.

Markets exhibit similar behavior. Investors' rewards are largely random: they depend on whether the market is up or down on any given day. Periodically, there is a really big reward. The more volatile the market is, the more this is amplified, so the periodic rewards in the cryptocurrency market can be huge and playing the market can become addictive. It's not long, though, before the market is playing you: the fate of a bad gambler.

You can avoid this by deciding on a clear, well-tested and well-thought-out strategy and executing it systematically, resisting distraction by the media circus. If you stick to your strategy, you can do well in cryptocurrency. If you hop from strategy to strategy or idea to idea or hot tip to hot tip, you will often suffer.

One approach is to use a buy-and-hold strategy, which we discussed in Chapter 5. That removes a lot

CRYPTOCURRENCY RISK MANAGEMENT

of the psychological turmoil of the decision-making process, but increases stress from market movements. Remember that buy and hold is frequently not comfortable for people in the cryptocurrency market, where a position can lose up to 90% of its value, but your goal as family wealth manager is to find an investment strategy that suits the family's psychology as opposed to searching for the absolute best answer in mathematical terms. This is a good time to re-read the chapters in Part One and ask yourself: "Why am I creating a cryptocurrency allocation in my family's portfolio? What role does it serve? Why am I doing this for my family? What am I hoping for my family to gain by doing this?"

TO MITIGATE

- Remember an investment strategy must work for the investor first.
- Be thoughtful about the total portfolio impact when allocating capital.
- Select a strategy that works for you and stick to it.

Risk: The dangers of strategic drift

There are so many winning strategies to choose from, many of which we examined in Chapter 5. The key is to decide on one and stick to the decision.

Strategic drift happens when you start out with a particular investment strategy, but over time drift into others because you think there's a better opportunity over there or those different strategies are outperforming yours at a given moment. In other words, you leap from whatever's hot to whatever's hot. The problem is that whatever's hot now wasn't hot a few minutes ago or a few days ago or a few months ago. Whatever's going to be hot next probably isn't hot today.

You end up playing a giant game of Whac-A-Mole with your asset managers and investing strategy instead of having a thoughtful, disciplined approach. I encourage you instead to think about what each strategy adds to your portfolio and, crucially, look at the correlation between the strategies. This handy family cryptocurrency strategy checklist will help:

- What is the goal of allocating to cryptocurrencies (usually growth)?

- What assets will we include in the portfolio (top-tier, speculative, DeFi, NFTs)?

- How will we weight the holdings in our portfolio?

- How will we manage custody (self-custody versus third party)?

- How will we preserve capital in down markets or if some of our holdings drop to zero?

- How will we acquire the cryptocurrency?

- What portfolio weight will we give our cryptocurrency allocation?

- Who will manage the business continuity for the portfolio?

With the answers to these questions in mind, you can build a cryptocurrency allocation that serves your family rather than the many unscrupulous actors in the industry. Of the numerous strategies available, two of them may seem interesting, so it may be sensible to allocate to both.

Depending on your goals, a digital asset allocation approximating 70% momentum and 30% mean reversion may be just as appropriate as another family's 50% buy and hold, 25% arbitrage, 25% VC approach. Rather than chasing the strategy presented to you, pursue strategies intentionally and deliberately, constructing an allocation that works in up and down markets. It's a philosophical approach: deciding to hold firm through turbulence rather than jumping from strategy to strategy. When the pendulum swings back the other way, if you have been consistent with your strategic planning, you will participate in your strategy's growth.

Many family offices and high net-worth individuals will choose not to manage their cryptocurrency allocation directly and rely instead on asset managers. You will need to verify that your asset manager has the deep knowledge, software and infrastructure to help you execute your strategy and maintain it through good times and bad. It's important, of course, to hire someone you can trust. There is a guide to hiring an asset manager in the Appendix.

TO MITIGATE

- Stand firm with your strategy rather than jumping from one to another.
- Use the family cryptocurrency strategy checklist to help you find the strategy or strategies that fit your family's needs.
- It may be that your best course of action is to allocate to more than one strategy.
- If you choose to work with an asset manager, be sure to consult the guidance on how to choose one outlined in the Appendix.

Risk: Kidnapping

This is not a common risk, but it happens. Because cryptocurrencies are bearer assets and the transactions are immensely difficult to unwind, it is an excellent method of payment for criminals. If your loved ones are kidnapped and you withdraw a million dollars in cash, the bank is going to ask questions, but if you send a million dollars in cryptocurrency across the internet, no one is the wiser and the money is gone forever. Another scenario is the kidnapper makes the victim give up their keys so they can then transfer the assets anywhere on the blockchain to an address they own, which will be almost impossible to trace.

In the world of physical cash, there are a few ways to trace payments such as marking bills, but we don't have that option in the cryptocurrency world yet. We do have the concept of tainted addresses, when credible exchanges do not accept cryptocurrencies from addresses that are known to have been part of a criminal enterprise such as kidnapping, but that is not a serious deterrent because the cryptocurrency can still be sold on the black market.

There have been instances of people being kidnapped after being too public with their large crypto holdings. As well as managing the risks outlined in this book, you must be modest about your crypto holdings. If people don't know you have it, they are not going to come after you for it. This is another good reason to use high-quality third-party custody providers or asset managers to hold coins for you and to distribute coins across multiple exchanges to keep your profile a little lower.

TO MITIGATE

- Be modest about your crypto holdings.
- Use third-party custody holders or asset managers so you are not holding your cryptocurrencies yourself.
- Distribute coins across multiple exchanges.
- If using self-custody, lock the keys away from yourself across multiple locations so even you don't have access to them without significant delays.

Risk: The $5 wrench problem

There's a famous cartoon from the online comic *XKCD*[61] in which a criminal doesn't have a supercomputer to crack the target's fantastic security, so decides to buy a $5 wrench and keep hitting the target until they give up the password.[62] This light-hearted cartoon serves to highlight a real and sinister risk. Because you exist somewhere in the physical world, there is always a risk that someone can physically force you to give up your keys or send them your cryptocurrencies. You can't eliminate this risk, but you can construct layer upon layer of protection.

Besides flying under the radar, you can help yourself by revoking your own access to the cryptocurrencies. Throughout this book, we've talked about using hardware wallets. If the keys are on the hardware wallet and the wallet is securely stored, the criminals have little to gain through physical attacks.

By creating obstacles for yourself when you want to access your own keys, you're creating obstacles for others.

If someone attacks you in the middle of the night and you have your keys in a vault that's only open during the day, then they have to wait until tomorrow. You can't walk into the private vault or the bank where you keep your keys in a safe deposit box with someone holding a gun to your head; security will notice. Earlier in the book, we talked about not keeping all your keys in one site and partitioning keys in different sites. If there are enough obstacles, common sense will often prevail and the criminal will look for an easier target.

You want to be a harder target than the next person for those who want to steal from you. While you can never be perfectly safe, you can improve your safety tremendously by being careful.

TO MITIGATE

- Make it as difficult as possible to gain access to your keys. This difficulty can act as a huge deterrent to those who wish to rob you.
- Keep a low profile. Do not advertise your crypto holdings.

Summary

In this chapter, we have looked at the risks inherent in us all—being human. These include the psychological strain the market can have on us and the temptation to jump from one hot strategy to the next, but we have to remember that what's hot now in the crypto world may not be hot in five minutes, let alone tomorrow.

We also looked at the more sinister risks to high net-worth families and individuals of kidnapping and other physical attacks by those wishing to gain access to our cryptocurrencies. While we cannot completely eliminate these risks, we can lessen the chances of them happening by making sure we never reveal our cryptocurrency holdings publicly.

This brings us to the end of the Cryptocurrency Risk Primer. Follow the advice held within the chapters of Part Two and you stand as good a chance as possible of guarding against the many risks just waiting for the unsuspecting crypto investor.

Conclusion

Cryptocurrency is an emerging asset class, so the threats are also emerging. This book has covered the important threats that we know of today, but there will undoubtedly be more in the near future as cryptocurrencies evolve and grow and new products are created. Today's analysis of risk won't be comprehensive, but it is as comprehensive as it can be at this time.

The future-proof mitigation strategy is to stay up to date and informed about emerging threats. You need to know the sort of detail that you won't read in the papers until it's too late, for example whether a certain blockchain project has absconded with any user funds lately. This is difficult because there's so much misinformation out there and few high-quality news sources about cryptocurrency.

Remember that half the messages on message boards or articles about cryptocurrency in newspapers are released to move the price because market manipulation is legal in the crypto world. It's best to decide on your strategy, stick to it and ignore the news, while being aware of what is happening with specific projects, their development roadmaps and the general participation of the project's community. You (or your asset manager) will have to monitor and engage with the projects, which means reading development message boards and being involved in the developer communities. You might not get a straight answer, but you'll learn about the different schools of thought. After educating yourself, you'll be better placed to make up your own mind.

There isn't going to be an answer that's perfectly crafted for you because no one understands your risk tolerance like you do. The risk profile of a twenty-year-old in their dorm room who has $1,000 to invest and is hoping to catch the next hot coin will be different than a family office deploying multiple millions of dollars in capital that needs to be protected for future generations. If you manage family assets, you have to be more right than a young investor who's taken a loss of $10,000 or $1,000 that they're going to make back over the course of their career. These setbacks for family offices are more painful and more challenging because you are dealing with multi-generational timelines and losses matter more. It goes back to the key question: what is the purpose of holding cryptocurrency in your family's portfolio?

You need a high level of knowledge, skill and psychological stamina to manage family assets even with professional help; it's next to impossible alone. If you don't have an obvious asset manager in your family, you will need to hire one. The Appendix includes a checklist of questions for anyone you consider for this role.

My answer was to build my own. I manage TrueCode Capital, a cryptocurrency hedge fund that seeks to strike a balance between all the risks mentioned in this book and others as they emerge. The thesis of the fund is that if my family could survive the tremendous risks of the crypto market, the opportunity to prosper would be fantastic. I have now opened the strategy to other family offices and high net-worth individuals to invest alongside my family.

If you would like to learn more about the fund, go to www.truecodecapital.com/performance to download the fact sheet. If you'd like to stay abreast of future writings related to digital asset risk, visit www.truecodecapital.com/subscribe to be added to the email list.

APPENDIX

Hiring An Asset Manager

A good asset manager will understand these questions and answer them competently and confidently. If they don't know who their auditor is, for example, they're probably not a good fund manager.

Ask a prospective asset manager:

- Are you taking custody of the cryptocurrencies or using third-party custody (i.e. who's going to own the keys)?

- Who are your counterparties? Who's holding the coins for you? Who is your fund administrator? Your auditor? Who's running compliance for you? Are you using any exchanges that do not have SOC 2 compliance?

- Do you pair well with my overall portfolio strategy? (All strategies work better in some environments than others, so your asset manager should know what environments your preferred strategy works well in.)

- How did your strategy perform during the last bear market?

- What kind of tokens will you be exposing me to?

- What instruments are you using? Futures contracts? Are you holding the crypto tokens yourself? Are you buying ETFs? Trust accounts? Are you using leverage?

- Are you using stablecoins for cash positions? Which ones?

- What jurisdiction are you in? (You will need to consider if you will be able to sue them if it's not the same as yours.)

- Who are you insured by?

- Are you registered with the state or federal securities regulator (e.g. the SEC) in the US or an equivalent regulator elsewhere?

References

1   Reid, A, "Kodak file for bankruptcy – A lesson for all
    camera companies past and present" (EOSHD, 19 January
    2012), www.eoshd.com/news/kodak-file-for-bankruptcy-
    a-lesson-for-all-camera-companies-past-and-present,
    accessed 14 September 2022
2   Maiers, M, "The basics of SOC 2 compliance" (Logicgate, 3
    December 2020), www.logicgate.com/blog/the-basics-of-
    soc-2-compliance, accessed 14 September 2022
3   Feeley, J and Hull, D, "Elon Musk Says Shifting SolarCity
    Workers Helped Tesla Stay Afloat" (Bloomberg UK,
    30 October 2019), www.bloomberg.com/news/
    articles/2019-10-30/musk-said-shifting-solarcity-workers-
    helped-tesla-stay-afloat, accessed 26 September 2022
4   CFI Team, "Survivorship Bias" (CFI, 15 May 2020), https://
    corporatefinanceinstitute.com/resources/knowledge/
    other/survivorship-bias, accessed 14 September 2022
5   "Ponzi Schemes" (US Securities and Exchange
    Commission), www.investor.gov/protect-your-
    investments/fraud/types-fraud/ponzi-scheme, accessed
    14 September 2022

6   Dalio, R, *Principles for Dealing with the Changing World Order: Why nations succeed and fail* (Avid Reader Press/ Simon & Schuster, 2021)
7   Markowitz, H M, "Foundations of portfolio theory" (*The Journal of Finance*, 46(2), 469–477, 1991), https:// doi.org/10.1111/j.1540-6261.1991.tb02669.x, accessed 14 September 2022
Levy, H and Markowitz, H M, "Approximating expected utility by a function of mean and variance" (*American Economic Review*, 69(3), 308–317, 1979), www.jstor.org/ stable/1807366, accessed 14 September 2022
Markowitz, H M, "Investment for the long run: New evidence for an old rule" (*The Journal of Finance*, 31(5), 1273–1286, 1976), https://doi.org/10.1111/j.1540-6261.1976. tb03213.x , accessed 14 September 2022
Fabozzi, F. J, Gupta, F and Markowitz, H M, "The legacy of modern portfolio theory" (*Journal of Investing*, 11(3), 7–22, 2002), https://doi.org/10.3905/joi.2002.319510, accessed 14 September 2022
Markowitz, H, "Portfolio Selection" (*The Journal of Finance*, 7(1), 77–91, 1952), https://doi.org/10.1111/j.1540-6261.1952. tb01525.x, accessed 14 September 2022
8   Farrington, R, "What is a Boglehead and what investing lessons can you learn?" (The College Investor, 17 July 2022), https://thecollegeinvestor.com/4119/boglehead/, accessed 14 September 2022
9   CFI Team, "CAGR" (CFI, 6 February 2022), https:// corporatefinanceinstitute.com/resources/knowledge/ finance/what-is-cagr, accessed 26 September 2022
10 Market data from www.tradingview.com
11 @MicahZoltu, "Introduction to smart contracts" (Ethereum. org, 25 August 2022), https://ethereum.org/en/ developers/docs/smart-contracts, accessed 14 September 2022
12 Web3 Payments Working Group, www.w3.org/Payments/ WG, accessed 26 September 2022
13 Roberts, J. J, "Blockchain and the web are coming together, says Berners-Lee" (*Fortune*, 17 October 2017), https:// fortune.com/2017/10/17/blockchain-berners-lee, accessed 14 September 2022
14 Newman, M E J, *Mathematics of Networks* (iNetworks, Oxford: Oxford University Press, 2019), pp. 126–128

15 @wackerow, "Proof-of-Stake (POS)" (Ethereum.org, 2022), https://ethereum.org/en/developers/docs/consensus-mechanisms/pos, accessed 14 September 2022

16 @wackerow, "Proof-of-stake (POS)" (Ethereum.org, 2022), https://ethereum.org/en/developers/docs/consensus-mechanisms/pos, accessed 14 September 2022

17 "M2 monetary aggregate" (Federal Reserve Bank of St. Louis), www.stlouisfed.org/financial-crisis/data/m2-monetary-aggregate, accessed 14 September 2022

18 Board of Governors of the Federal Reserve System (US), M2 [M2SL], (FRED® Graphs ©Federal Bank of St Louis. 2022. All rights reserved. All FRED® Graphs appear courtesy of Federal Reserve Bank of St Louis), https://fred.stlouisfed.org/series/M2SL, accessed 16 May 2022

19 "Total circulating Bitcoin" (Blockchain.com), www.blockchain.com/charts/total-bitcoins, accessed 14 September 2022

20 Perrin, A, "16% of Americans say they have ever [sic] invested in, traded or used cryptocurrency" (Pew Research Center, 11 November 2021), www.pewresearch.org/fact-tank/2021/11/11/16-of-americans-say-they-have-ever-invested-in-traded-or-used-cryptocurrency, accessed 14 September 2022

21 CFI Team "Diffusion of innovation" (CFI, 24 April 2021), https://corporatefinanceinstitute.com/resources/knowledge/other/diffusion-of-innovation, accessed 14 September 2022

22 Board of Governors of the Federal Reserve System (US), "Market Yield on US Treasury Securities at 10-Year Constant Maturity [DGS10]" (FRED® Graphs ©Federal Bank of St Louis. 2022. All rights reserved. All FRED® Graphs appear courtesy of Federal Reserve Bank of St Louis), https://fred.stlouisfed.org/series/DGS10, accessed 16 May 2022

23 "Roosevelt's Gold Program, 1933" (Federal Reserve History, 22 November 2013), www.federalreservehistory.org/essays/roosevelts-gold-program

24 "Nixon Ends Convertibility of U.S. Dollars to Gold and Announces Wage/Price Controls, August 1971" (Federal Reserve History, 22 November 2013), www.federalreservehistory.org/essays/gold-convertibility-ends

25 US Bureau of Labor Statistics, "Producer price index by commodity: All commodities [PPIACO], (RED, FRED® Graphs ©Federal Bank of St Louis. 2022. All rights reserved. All FRED® Graphs appear courtesy of Federal Reserve Bank of St Louis), https://fred.stlouisfed.org/series/PPIACO, accessed 16 May 2022

26 Board of Governors of the Federal Reserve System (US), "Market Yield on US Treasury securities at 10-year constant maturity, quoted on an investment basis [DGS10]" (FRED® Graphs ©Federal Bank of St Louis. 2022. All rights reserved. All FRED® Graphs appear courtesy of Federal Reserve Bank of St Louis) https://fred.stlouisfed.org/series/DGS10, accessed 16 May 2022

27 US Office of Management and Budget and Federal Reserve Bank of St. Louis, "Federal debt: Total public debt as percent of gross domestic product [GFDEGDQ188S]" (FRED, Federal Reserve Bank of St. Louis) https://fred. stlouisfed.org/series/GFDEGDQ188S, accessed 16 May 2022

28 Musk, E (@elonmusk), "Tesla has suspended vehicle purchases using Bitcoin…" (Twitter, 12 May 2021), https://twitter.com/elonmusk/status/1392602041025843203?lang=en, accessed 14 September 2022

29 Musk, E (@elonmusk), "Bitcoin hashing (AKA mining) energy usage is starting to exceed…" (Twitter, 20 May 2021), https://twitter.com/elonmusk/status/1395472799020421120?ref_src=twsrc%5Etfw, accessed 14 September 2022

30 Musk, E (@elonmusk), "Spoke with North American Bitcoin miners…" (Twitter, 24 May 2021), https://twitter.com/elonmusk/status/1396914548167233537?lang=en, accessed 14 September 2022

31 Sigalos, M, "These 23-year-old Texans made $4 million last year mining bitcoin off flare gas from oil drilling" (CNBC, 12 February 2022), www.cnbc.com/2022/02/12/23-year-old-texans-made-4-million-mining-bitcoin-off-flared-natural-gas.html, accessed 26 September 2022

32 Shen, M, "How $60 Billion in Terra Coins Went Up in Algorithmic Smoke" (Bloomberg UK, 21 May 2022), www.bloomberg.com/graphics/2022-crypto-luna-terra-stablecoin-explainer, accessed 13 September 2022

33 "What is KYC" (SWIFT, no date), www.swift.com/
    your-needs/financial-crime-cyber-security/know-your-
    customer-kyc/meaning-kyc, accessed 13 September 2022

34 CME Group, "Bitcoin futures – contract specs", www.
    cmegroup.com/markets/cryptocurrencies/bitcoin/bitcoin.
    contractSpecs.html, accessed 14 September 2022

35 CME Group, "Bitcoin futures – contract specs", www.
    cmegroup.com/markets/cryptocurrencies/bitcoin/bitcoin.
    contractSpecs.html, accessed 13 September 2022

36 Eliazar, I, "Lindy's Law" (*Physica A: Statistical mechanics and
    its applications*, Volume 486, November 15
    2017, pp 797–805), https://doi.org/10.1016/j.
    physa.2017.05.077, accessed 6 October 2022

37 "Warren Buffett explains how he pays less taxes than his
    secretary" (YouTube, 12 January 2020), www.youtube.com/
    watch?v=J9Hg_e4NVpQ, accessed 14 September 2022

38 Calculated using historical inflation of 4% since 1971
    when the US abandoned the gold standard. Inflation Data
    from www.macrotrends.net. Market Data from www.
    tradingview.com.

39 Graham, B, *The Intelligent Investor* (Harper & Brothers, 1949)

40 Legal Information Institute, "Securities Act of 1933"
    (Cornell Law School), www.law.cornell.edu/wex/
    securities_act_of_1933, accessed
    13 September 2022

41 Legal Information Institute, "Securities Act of 1934"
    (Cornell Law School), www.law.cornell.edu/wex/
    securities_exchange_act_of_1934, accessed 13 September
    2022

42 "Roosevelt's Gold Program, 1933" (Federal Reserve History,
    22 November 2013), www.federalreservehistory.org/
    essays/roosevelts-gold-program, accessed 14 September
    2022

43 "Welcome to the Diem Project", www.diem.com/en-us,
    accessed 14 September 2022

44 Schroeder, P, Nair, S. S and Paul, K, "Facebook's Libra
    currency abandoned by major financial companies"
    (Reuters, 11 October 2019), www.reuters.com/article/us-
    facebook-cryptocurrency-ebay-idINKBN1WQ2KL, accessed
    14 September 2022

45 About Form 6781, Gains and losses from section 1256
    contracts and straddles (IRS), www.irs.gov/forms-pubs/
    about-form-6781, accessed 14 September 2022

46 Topic No. 409 Capital Gains and Losses (IRS), www.irs. gov/taxtopics/tc409, accessed 14 September 2022

47 Wilson, T and Singh, M, "Dogecoin watch out! 'Shiba inu' token muscles into cryptocurrency top 10" (Reuters, 28 October 2021), www.reuters.com/business/finance/ dogecoin-watch-out-shiba-inu-token-muscles-into-cryptocurrency-top-10-2021-10-28, accessed 3 October 2022

48 "Beyond Passwords: Simpler, Stronger Authentication with FIDO2" (FIDO Alliance, 15 November 2018), https:// fidoalliance.org/beyond-passwords-simpler-stronger-authentication-with-fido2, accessed 14 September 2022

49 Whitney, L, "SANS cybersecurity training firm suffers data breach due to phishing attack" (TechRepublic, 2020), www. techrepublic.com/article/sans-cybersecurity-training-firm-suffers-data-breach-due-to-phishing-attack, accessed 14 September 2022

50 Consumer Financial Protection Bureau, www. consumerfinance.gov, accessed 14 September 2022

51 Bureau of Consumer Protection (Federal Trade Commission), www.ftc.gov/about-ftc/bureaus-offices/ bureau-consumer-protection, accessed 14 September 2022

52 "Hacker Infects Node.js Package to Steal from Bitcoin Wallets" (Trend Micro, 29 November 2018), www. trendmicro.com/vinfo/it/security/news/cybercrime-and-digital-threats/hacker-infects-node-js-package-to-steal-from-bitcoin-wallets, accessed 13 September 2022

53 "Business Employment Dynamics" (US Bureau of Labor Statistics), www.bls.gov/bdm/entrepreneurship/ entrepreneurship.htm, accessed 13 September 2022

54 Kharif, A, "Mt. Gox creditors inch closer to repayment as Bitcoin dump looms" (Bloomberg UK, 2022), www. bloomberg.com/news/articles/2022-07-07/mt-gox-creditors-inch-closer-to-repayment-as-bitcoin-dump-looms, accessed 14 September 2022

55 Ghosh, S and Shukla, S, "Crypto Debacle at Celsius Rattles Market Already Shaken by Terra" (Bloomberg News, 13 June 2022), https://news.bloombergtax.com/crypto/ crypto-lender-celsius-stops-withdrawals-fuels-market-slump-1, accessed 13 September 2022

56 Hill, J, "Coinbase lets users know what a bankruptcy could mean for their crypto" (Bloomberg UK, 2022), www.bloomberg.com/news/articles/2022-05-11/coinbase-gives-256-billion-reminder-about-agonies-of-bankruptcy#xj4y7vz, accessed 13 September 2022

57 "LUNA Market Update May 2022" (Truecode Capital, 11 May 2022), https://truecodecapital.com/luna-market-update-may-2022, accessed 22 November 2022

58 John, A, "Stablecoin Terra's broken dollar peg hits wider crypto markets" (Reuters, 10 May 2022), www.reuters.com/business/finance/stablecoin-terras-broken-dollar-peg-hits-wider-crypto-markets-2022-05-10, accessed 22 November 2022

59 Kharif, O, "CryptoKitties Mania Overwhelms Ethereum Network's Processing" (Bloomberg UK, 4 December 2017), www.bloomberg.com/news/articles/2017-12-04/cryptokitties-quickly-becomes-most-widely-used-ethereum-app#xj4y7vzkg, accessed 14 September 2022

60 "Token Migration" (Kin, no date), https://kin.org/token-migration, accessed 14 September 2022

61 Used under creative commons license. https://xkcd.com/538

62 XKCD Security, https://xkcd.com/538, accessed 14 September 2022

Acknowledgments

When it comes to opportunities for gratitude, I am happy to say I have an embarrassment of riches.

I would especially like to thank the TrueCode Capital team: Jeffrey Fidelman, the singularly most effective person I've ever encountered; Michael Stellwagen, whose sage guidance has been indispensable; and Karen Tiber Leland, whose branding wizardry kicked off this entire project.

Thank you to a very good friend who introduced me to "this interesting project called Bitcoin" so many years ago.

A special acknowledgment to the Denver TIGER21 community, especially Douglas Johnson and Elizabeth Ledoux whose encouragement helped launch this project.

A very special thank-you to the love of my life, Aimee; the heart and soul of our family.

My blessings are beyond measure.

The Author

Joshua M. Peck is the founder of TrueCode Capital, which aims to provide asymmetric growth for family offices and high net-worth families by creating a risk-managed exposure to the long-term growth in the emerging cryptocurrency market. Drawing on nearly twenty years of experience developing and capitalizing on emerging technologies, he utilizes a systems approach to portfolio management that leverages his deep quantitative background in financial engineering, machine learning and applied mathematics.

Early in his career, Joshua worked in academia in support of high-performance research computing environments where he became a regional expert in systems engineering, cybersecurity and data engineering. Soon thereafter, he co-founded as chief technology officer an internet start-up that quickly grew to $30million in revenue.

Josh is a guest of the media and has been featured in *The Wall Street Journal, The Guardian, Entrepreneur,* CBS MoneyWatch, and Bloomberg.

In addition to his work, he has been active in philanthropy through the Denver Mile High Rotary Foundation, where he served as treasurer and member of the World Community Service committee. Joshua has also served as an advisory board member, angel investor and mentor for various venture clubs and accelerators, and has invested in a diverse group of companies.

Joshua received his B.S. in Computer Science from Pittsburg State University and his Master of Science, Engineering Management from the University of Kansas. He resides with his family in Fort Collins, Colorado where he is creating a first-generation family office to care for his descendants for many generations to come.

⊕ www.joshuampeck.com

▥ www.linkedin.com/in/joshua--peck

▣ https://twitter.com/joshpeck

Proceeds from sales of this book will be donated to The Foundation for Digital Asset Risk (FDAR), a non-profit organisation I founded to educate the greater investment community about the risks of investing in digital assets and to help the broader world invest in crypto more safely. You can learn more at www.fdar.org.